Access, Resource Sharing and Collection Development

Access, Resource Sharing and Collection Development

Sul H. Lee
Editor

The Haworth Press, Inc.
New York

Access, Resource Sharing and Collection Development has also been published as *Journal of Library Administration*, Volume 22, Number 4 1996.

The development, preparation, and publication of this work has been undertaken with great care. However, the publisher, employees, editors, and agents of The Haworth Press and all imprints of The Haworth Press, Inc., including The Haworth Medical Press and Pharmaceutical Products Press, are not responsible for any errors contained herein or for consequences that may ensue from use of materials or information contained in this work. Opinions expressed by the author(s) are not necessarily those of The Haworth Press, Inc.

The Haworth Press, Inc., 10 Alice Street, Binghamton, NY 13904-1580 USA

Library of Congress Cataloging-in-Publication Data

Access, resource sharing and collection development / Sul H. Lee, editor.
    p. cm.
    "Access, resource sharing and collection development has also been published as Journal of library administration, volume 22, number 4 1996"–Verso t.p.
    Includes bibliographical references and index.
    ISBN 1-56024-811-4 (alk. paper)
    1. Collection development (Libraries)–United States–Congresses. 2. Document delivery–United States–Congresses. I. Lee, Sul H.
Z687.2.U6A28 1996
025.2'1–dc20
                                               96-23321
                                                CIP

INDEXING & ABSTRACTING

Contributions to this publication are selectively indexed or abstracted in print, electronic, online, or CD-ROM version(s) of the reference tools and information services listed below. This list is current as of the copyright date of this publication. See the end of this section for additional notes.

- *Academic Abstracts/CD-ROM,* EBSCO Publishing, P.O. Box 2250, Peabody, MA 01960-7250

- *Academic Search: data base of 2,000 selected academic serials; updated monthly,* EBSCO Publishing, 83 Pine Street, Peabody, MA 01960

- *AGRICOLA Database,* National Agricultural Library, 10301 Baltimore Boulevard, Room 002, Beltsville, MD 20705

- *Cambridge Scientific Abstracts, Health & Safety Science Abstracts*, Environmental Routenet (accessed via INTERNET), 7200 Wisconsin Avenue #601, Bethesda, MD 20814

- *CNPIEC Reference Guide: Chinese National Directory of Foreign Periodicals,* P.O. Box 88, Beijing, People's Republic of China

- *Current Articles on Library Literature and Services (CALLS),* Pakistan Library Association, Quaid-e-Azam Library, Bagh-e-Jinnah, Lahore, Pakistan

- *Current Awareness Bulletin,* Association for Information Management, Information House, 20-24 Old Street, London EC1V 9AP, England

- *Current Index to Journals in Education,* Syracuse University, 4-194 Center for Science and Technology, Syracuse, NY 13244-4100

(continued)

- *Educational Administration Abstracts (EAA),* Sage Publications, Inc., 2455 Teller Road, Newbury Park, CA 91320

- *Higher Education Abstracts,* Claremont Graduate School, 231 East Tenth Street, Claremont, CA 91711

- *IBZ International Bibliography of Periodical Literature,* Zeller Verlag GmbH & Co., P.O.B. 1949, d-49009 Osnabruck, Germany

- *Index to Periodical Articles Related to Law,* University of Texas, 727 East 26th Street, Austin, TX 78705

- *Information Reports & Bibliographies,* Science Associates International, Inc., 6 Hastings Road, Marlboro, NJ 07746-1313

- *Information Science Abstracts,* Plenum Publishing Company, 233 Spring Street, New York, NY 10013-1578

- *Informed Librarian, The,* Infosources Publishing, 140 Norma Road, Teaneck, NJ 07666

- *INSPEC Information Services,* Institution of Electrical Engineers, Michael Faraday House, Six Hills Way, Stevenage, Herts SG1 2AY, England

- *INTERNET ACCESS (& additional networks) Bulletin Board for Libraries ("BUBL"), coverage of information resources on INTERNET, JANET, and other networks.*
  - JANET X.29: UK.AC.BATH.BUBL or 00006012101300
  - TELNET: BUBL.BATH.AC.UK or 138.38.32.45 login 'bubl'
  - Gopher: BUBL.BATH.AC.UK (138.32.32.45). Port 7070
  - World Wide Web: http: / / www.bubl.bath.ac.uk./BUBL/ home.html
  - NISSWAIS: telnetniss.ac.uk (for the NISS gateway)
  The Andersonian Library, Curran Building, 101 St. James Road, Glasgow G4 ONS, Scotland

(continued)

- *Journal of Academic Librarianship: Guide to Professional Literature,* The Belmont Group, 1700 E. Elliot Road, 6-512, Tempe, AZ

- *Konyvtari Figyelo-Library Review,* National Szechenyi Library, Centre for Library and Information Science, 4-1827 Budapest, Hungary

- *Library & Information Science Abstracts (LISA),* Bowker-Saur Limited, Maypole House, Maypole Road, East Grinstead, West Sussex RH19 1HH, England

- *Library Literature,* The H.W. Wilson Company, 950 University Avenue, Bronx, NY 10452

- *MasterFILE: updated database from EBSCO Publishing,* 83 Pine Street, Peabody, MA 01960

- *Newsletter of Library and Information Services,* China Sci-Tech Book Review, Library of Academia Sinica, 8 Kexueyuan Nanlu, Zhongguancun, Beijing 100080, People's Republic of China

- *OT BibSys,* American Occupational Therapy Foundation, P.O. Box 31220, Rockville, MD 20824-1220

- *PASCAL International Bibliography T205: Sciences de l'information Documentation,* INIST/CNRS-Service Gestion des Documents Primaries, 2, Allee du Parc de Brabois, F-54514 Vandoeuvre-les-Nancy, Cedex, France

- *Public Affairs Information Bulletin (PAIS),* Public Affairs Information Service, Inc., 521 West 43rd Street, New York, NY 10036-4396

- *Referativnyi Zhurnal (Abstracts Journal of the Institute of Scientific Information of the Republic of Russia),* The Institute of Scientific Information, Baltijskaja ul., 14, Moscow A-219, Republic of Russia

- *Trade & Industry Index,* Information Access Company, 362 Lakeside Drive, Foster City, CA 94404

(continued)

SPECIAL BIBLIOGRAPHIC NOTES

related to special journal issues (separates)
and indexing/abstracting

☐ indexing/abstracting services in this list will also cover material in any "separate" that is co-published simultaneously with Haworth's special thematic journal issue or DocuSerial. Indexing/abstracting usually covers material at the article/chapter level.

☐ monographic co-editions are intended for either non-subscribers or libraries which intend to purchase a second copy for their circulating collections.

☐ monographic co-editions are reported to all jobbers/wholesalers/approval plans. The source journal is listed as the "series" to assist the prevention of duplicate purchasing in the same manner utilized for books-in-series.

☐ to facilitate user/access services all indexing/abstracting services are encouraged to utilize the co-indexing entry note indicated at the bottom of the first page of each article/chapter/contribution.

☐ this is intended to assist a library user of any reference tool (whether print, electronic, online, or CD-ROM) to locate the monographic version if the library has purchased this version but not a subscription to the source journal.

☐ individual articles/chapters in any Haworth publication are also available through the Haworth Document Delivery Services (HDDS).

For Melissa

ABOUT THE EDITOR

Sul H. Lee, Dean of the University Libraries, University of Oklahoma, is an internationally recognized leader and consultant in the library administration and management field. Dean Lee is a past member of the Board of Directors, Association of Research Libraries, the ARL Office of Management Services Advisory Committee, and the Council for the American Library Association. His works include *The Impact of Rising Costs of Serials and Monographs on Library Services and Programs; Library Material Costs and Access to Information; Budgets for Acquisitions: Strategies for Serials, Monographs, and Electronic Formats; Vendor Evaluation and Acquisition Budgets; Collection Assessment and Acquisitions Budgets; The Role and Future of Special Collections in Research Libraries; Declining Acquisitions Budgets;* and *Access, Ownership, and Resource Sharing.* He is also Editor of the *Journal of Library Administration* and *Collection Management.*

Access, Resource Sharing
and Collection Development

CONTENTS

∞ ALL HAWORTH BOOKS AND JOURNALS
ARE PRINTED ON CERTIFIED
ACID-FREE PAPER

Introduction

For over a decade the University of Oklahoma Libraries in conjunction with the University of Oklahoma Foundation have sponsored an annual conference examining the important library issues of the day. On March 2 and 3, 1995 this tradition was continued with the conference entitled, "Access, Resource Sharing and Collection Development." This conference extended the investigation and discussion of issues about the role of libraries in acquiring, storing and disseminating information in different formats.

George Shipman, University Librarian at the University of Oregon, begins the discussion with an examination of challenges facing academic libraries and the library profession. The competition for limited resources and the need to develop competent librarians are two major issues facing our profession. Connie McCarthy, Associate University Librarian at Duke University, continues with an article reflecting on the current issues in collection management. She highlights some of the changes in collection management and the future role of the bibliographer.

Charles Hamaker, Assistant Dean for Collection Development at Louisiana State University, offers insight into the role and activities of the research libraries using studies from LSU. Mr. Hamaker sees the changing role of the Academy having significant influence on how libraries conduct business. Rebecca Lenzini, President of CARL Corporation, follows with an analysis of trends in document delivery. Her article presents an interesting discourse on many of the issues related to document delivery.

Ann Okerson, Director, Association of Research Libraries Office

[Haworth co-indexing entry note]: "Introduction." Lee, Sul H. Co-published simultaneously in *Journal of Library Administration* (The Haworth Press, Inc.) Vol. 22, No. 4, 1996, pp. 1-2; and: *Access, Resource Sharing and Collection Development* (ed: Sul H. Lee) The Haworth Press, Inc., 1996, pp. 1-2. Single or multiple copies of this article are available from The Haworth Document Delivery Service [1-800-342-9678, 9:00 a.m. - 5:00 p.m. (EST). E-mail address: getinfo@haworth.com].

of Scientific and Academic Publishing, examines the issue of copyright focusing on the work of the NII Working Group on Copyright and the Texaco copyright court case. Ms. Okerson discusses the current law and looks at the impact of electronic access upon it.

Anthony Ferguson, Associate University Librarian at Columbia University, explores the use of commercial document delivery services in libraries. He discusses a multitude of issues including the speed of delivery, the breadth of coverage, access versus ownership, and responsibility for cost recovery. Julia Ann Kelly follows with a description of "free" resources available on the Internet. In her article she discusses how resources are discovered and methods of evaluation. Joseph J. Fitzsimmons, Chairman of UMI, concludes the conference presentations with descriptions of the different options for document delivery and considerations in selecting document delivery products. He outlines some of the developments in remote access and CD-ROM products and puts forth selection criteria.

The success of the conference might well be judged by the reaction to the papers presented in this volume. The conference sessions included wonderful discussion, that unfortunately is not recorded in this publication. It is hoped continued debate and further investigation will continue as a result of this volume.

I would like to thank Donald Hudson for his efforts as Coordinator of the University of Oklahoma Libraries Conference, Wilbur Stolt for his editorial assistance, and Melanie Davidson for her secretarial contributions. Their help has made this conference and publication a much easier task.

Sul H. Lee

Fueling the Fires of Scholarship in the 90's

George W. Shipman

When Sul Lee first asked that I speak at this meeting, I confess that I was both flattered and a bit awed at the prospect of speaking to this gathering. I hope to share with you a perspective that you will find reasonable and one that will augment the wisdom you gain from the speakers who follow me in this program. It is a distinguished group that I have joined for this program and I am grateful for the opportunity to participate. Sul and I talked at some length over a pleasant dinner about the subject matter for this event: Access, resource-sharing and collection development in the twenty-first century. As we talked about the conference my mind began to race about graphic illustrations I might use in my presentation. I don't use overhead projections, but since they seem to be mandatory these days I brought one quote I thought appropriately matched the subject of this conference:

> More than any other time in history, mankind faces a crossroads. One path leads to despair and utter hopelessness. The other, to total extinction. Let us pray we have the wisdom to choose correctly.

–Woody Allen

George W. Shipman is University Librarian at The University of Oregon in Eugene, OR.

[Haworth co-indexing entry note]: "Fueling the Fires of Scholarship in the 90's." Shipman, George W. Co-published simultaneously in *Journal of Library Administration* (The Haworth Press, Inc.) Vol. 22, No. 4, 1996, pp. 3-13; and: *Access, Resource Sharing and Collection Development* (ed: Sul H. Lee) The Haworth Press, Inc., 1996, pp. 3-13. Single or multiple copies of this article are available from The Haworth Document Delivery Service [1-800-342-9678, 9:00 a.m. - 5:00 p.m. (EST). E-mail address: getinfo @haworth.com].

After agreeing to serve as the "warm up act" for the remaining speakers I made a flurry of notes that I hoped would guide me in the writing of my presentation. That process consumed most of my return flight in the confinement of a coach class seat winging my way back to Oregon. I was rather proud of my degree of organization and smugly put my notes aside for a few days' germination. Those notes served as the précis contained in the flyer used to drum up attendance at this conference. Later, I called Sul and asked for a list of the participants and the drafts of their précis, just for background information. After receiving his return mail and reading the tantalizing descriptions, I realized that I probably ought to be the wrap-up speaker if I was going to live and die by my original outline of organization because each of the speakers had listed (in their précis) most of the elements that I had planned on using in my remarks.

At first I was crestfallen to make this discovery, but then I realized that (1) Sul had simply put together all of the right ideas to be covered by this meeting, and (2) he had assembled a group of speakers who possessed an amazing level of prescience or perspicacity because they were obviously on the same wavelength as I! I might add that after thinking about the situation just a little more, this would be the first time that I have had the chance to introduce elements that ensuing speakers intend to address instead of the other way around. I don't think anything I say will deter my fellow speakers from their well-considered comments, but it is a comfortable position to be in for a change.

For the last few years we have heard a great deal of rhetoric about the library of the twenty-first century and the many marvels that we librarians will proffer to our patrons when we cross that momentous point in time. I agree with most of these prophesies and look forward to a delightful and fruitful future–a future based on the groundwork our profession has laid over the last twenty years. However, I contend that we have ten years of work to do during the remaining five years of this century, and I'd like to take this opportunity to talk about some of the things librarians need to accomplish during this crucial window of opportunity.

Of course I'm speaking to you as a director of a research library. This coming spring I will have completed twenty-eight years as a librarian. All of my service has been in the research library sector. With the exception of almost four years at the Library of Congress, all of my time has been spent as an academic library administrator. Over the course of this conference you will hear about specific strategies for information sharing. *My* main concern is to put together a complete plan of action to move library services forward into the next century, and then to figure out *how* to transform such an ambitious plan into reality. My thoughts today will focus on the challenges of *how* to get from strategic plan to real accomplishment. These challenges include the politics of scarce resource allocation, the struggle to redefine our profession and to broaden our vision, and finally, the need for a strong and effective program of advocacy.

Before I talk about hurdles, pitfalls, and other obstacles in the road, I'd like to take a few minutes to acknowledge the strong and forward-thinking work many of you have contributed to get us where we are today. Research libraries now offer greatly improved forms of access to locally-held, traditionally formatted library materials. We have used evolving technologies to make available our holdings and those of other libraries. Additionally, we have provided access to material beyond the traditional formats out there on the wonderful World Wide Web. In spite of the fact that we often complain bitterly to one another that we have been hindered by the absence of resources, campus leaders who don't understand us, vendors who are slow to respond, etc., etc., I believe that librarians have made extraordinarily good use of time and resources to plan and implement remarkably effective information service tools. We have collaborated in consortia to utilize technology to link our holdings and to create protocols for service–all of which have served citizens, faculty and students well. The point of all of this is to suggest that the technological applications we have created have established an extraordinarily solid platform from which to launch each successive campaign of achievement and innovation. Additionally, these activities have created a profession that is highly literate and functional from a technological point of view.

And so we enter into the last few years of this century with two decades of solid work behind us. Now to the challenges I spoke of.

The first challenge comes under the heading of "allocating

scarce resources." The university research library is often engaged in a struggle to remain the primary repository for information resources. In the age of electronic media this will be truer than ever. In the near future we will confront again and again an old adversary dressed in new hi-tech togs–the cyber-version of the "boot leg" library–that is, the maverick collection now in electronic form, created and maintained by the academic department. This maverick is feared and loathed because it is typically outside the control of those who understand the care and feeding of library collections– namely, librarians. Time and again we have fought its creation, pointed out its redundancy, taken it over when we could, and, hav- ing taken it into our fold, smugly made it into an honest library. I've done this a few times myself, and if I have made light of attitudes and behavior, I'm merely pointing my finger at myself. Why did we feel so strongly about the bootleg library? Because we embrace the article of faith that the information business in the academy has rightfully been the responsibility of the Library and we know that most institutions can't afford to support redundant collections. Unfortunately, these maverick collections are almost always mis- construed by patrons to represent the institution's primary collec- tion serving the discipline. Since they are usually duplicative as well as incomplete, it's inevitable that the library is criticized for their flaws and deficiencies. There are, of course, exceptions to this rule.

The cybernetic version, the "bootleg information or data center," presents a more formidable challenge. Information was "discov- ered" in the late eighties or early nineties by faculty, computing centers, and university administrators, and now we have to worry about a proliferation of data centers which duplicate library-based resources and programs. They almost always, like their predeces- sors, serve very narrow slices of the institutional community, mini- mizing the value of the investment for broader constituencies. Such electronic information centers are justified by some members of the academy because they no longer believe in the "gateway" role of the library (or have forgotten about our successes!). Some see easy, quick solutions to short-term needs and have less concern than the Library for the long-term effects on overall institutional commit- ment to these expensive and valuable commodities.

And so we must restate all the old arguments defending the library as the logical central manager and repository for *all* forms of information. In some respects I see this as an uphill battle, since the possession of such glamorous electronic resources usually represents a badge of honor for its possessor, and since some provosts may have difficulty biting the bullet and placing the bulk of these resources under the aegis of the library. But in the face of these realities, the battle is winnable. We must remain steadfast in our claim that the institution's first obligation is to fund the larger enterprise, the library. We serve the largest possible clientele, the faculty and student body on a global scale. The library must remain the central repository for these expensive resources in order to optimize the institutional investment. After the library's claims have been met, other information requirements can be considered. This decision rests upon the consciences of its decision makers! I realize that I'm preaching to the converted–but this battle will heat up even more in the next five years. Now I must–we must–bring this message back to campus–persuasively, persistently, and without delay!

The battle for the electronic resource dollar will be fought in a series of skirmishes against the backdrop of the ongoing struggle to preserve the library's basic budget for operations and capital investment. In brief, we have successfully sold information technology as a way to leverage scarce materials resources. In fact we have been too successful. In the coming five years we must defend the library facility against the charge of obsolescence. We will do this by defending the value of printed materials and other, less than cutting edge, formats, both as the record of our culture and as an enduringly attractive format for communication. And we will also redefine the library as a teaching center for information literacy.

Library collections and resource managers have had a rocky ride for a long time now. In spite of the fact that most of our acquisitions budgets continue to grow in terms of real dollars, we have experienced a declining buying power because of inflation, a weakened dollar in foreign markets, increased publishing costs and, in at least some cases, excessive price increases. At the same time publishing in practically all disciplines has expanded, and new disciplines have emerged to swell scholarly production. This groundswell of creativity is naturally fueled by the promotion and tenure process. I haven't forgotten the compounding effect of the phenomenal increases in costs for scholarly journals, which far outstrips rate increases for monographs. The cumulative effect of these phenomena has been devastating over the course of the past two decades.

Unfortunately, or fortunately, depending upon your perspective, we have not seen a decline in demand from our patrons that might reduce the sting of these developments! Indeed, all reports show continued demand from our clientele. None of this is news to you. You are the ones who have been charged with figuring out how to use technology to share scarce resources, and to connect communities and collections. And in the process, you have helped to reshape our profession. We have become a cadre of well informed and supremely well organized professionals who are not intimidated by heretofore unknown or nonexistent information service issues.

But while we have used technology so successfully to leverage our resources, inevitably there is a cost. We have created an expectation that technology will replace the traditional library. There is an element of wishful thinking in this. Most of our buildings are either full or have predictable life spans and it's only natural that many academic administrators will be tempted to claim that we no longer need building programs because technology will render the book and journal obsolete. Further, technology has neatly dealt with the problems of time and space in that scholars can now obtain access to literature, data, and information at any time of any day from any telecommunications link. If you hear words to that effect, tell the speaker to take another, more responsible or objective look at the library and its staff. The current holdings of the University of Oregon Library have a replacement value of more than $130 million dollars, not counting our special collections. The scholarly value of any library collection is probably impossible to quantify. This represents a major cultural and economic investment, and most management types understand that you don't walk away from that level of capital investment.

Furthermore, we aren't at all sure when or if that technological marvel, the book, will be truly and completely replaced by newer forms of technology. We will continue to purchase traditionally formatted materials because they continue to be invaluable to most of our users. Moreover, many disciplines are still very poorly served by evolving technology. In short, we can predict our rate of growth in collections, and therefore spatial requirements, for at least ten plus years–and must plan for it accordingly.

And so this in summary is challenge number one–a thorny political problem. Libraries are expensive things to run, and getting more expensive with each passing year. Our management successes, achieved through sleek information technologies, have set up expectations of cost savings which we cannot meet. The Dean of the Library is therefore the bearer of bad news to the university president and the provost. We have a lot of explaining to do, and we must be persuasive. And so we promote, defend, and advocate for what is to all librarians and many, if not most of our patrons, the most vital component of any rational plan for the coming information age: the Library as the academy's primary information resource.

The second challenge I want to talk about is a challenge to our profession. Our facilities must now accommodate the equipment, systems, and people necessary to fulfill an expanded role in teaching information technology. Not long ago it was easy to say that your "generic" academic reference librarian was responsible for a combination of desk, or reference, service, book selection by virtue of some degree of subject specialization and subsequent liaison responsibility with academic departments, and perhaps, a share of instruction in the fine art of using the catalog and the reference collection. Today's picture is quite different in most of our libraries. Subject specialization has been expanded beyond knowledge of specific disciplines to include knowledge of the "map" of the technological universe and awareness of the resources serving those disciplines within that universe. Possession of this knowledge is imperative if we are to fulfill our traditional role within the scholarly process—that of gatekeeper. But now we are–or should be–more than gatekeepers, we are teachers. Libraries that have been successful in maintaining their position in the minds and hearts of the faculty and students they serve have eagerly embraced responsibility for teaching information technology. Our successful library models boast electronic classrooms in which librarians teach both students and faculty to use information resources. Additionally, they support library technology centers which provide direct access to networking, multimedia, and whatever got marketed yesterday afternoon.

Librarians remain aware of "it," they teach "it," they provide access to "it," they possess "it," they organize "it," and they market "it." Of course there is always the handful of academicians precariously perched on the horizon sneering at the rest of the world because they have made use of the most recently discovered black hole in this information-techno-universe. Let them have their arrogance. We have an obligation as librarians to provide the broadest possible means of access for our patrons to the farthest reaches in our information-techno-universe as possible. We must always strive to nudge higher our threshold of access, as well as that of our users. We are the broad brush painting the largest possible canvas.

But while we foster the evolution of an expanded role for librarians as teachers of information technology, we should not overlook the graduate library and information science programs which generated most of us. Some of these programs have been engaged in a profound revision of the curriculum. We should pay close attention to these efforts and strive to influence the proposed changes in creative and visionary ways, at the same time we improve and expand the staff development and continuing education programs for current practitioners. I am personally concerned about the need to systematically ascertain our professional continuing education needs and to do more for our current cadre in this respect. We can't encourage our professional graduate programs to modify the skills and training of their graduates if we are not committed to the formal retrofitting of current professionals in order to maintain equitable relationships and professional capacities.

At the same time, as our profession evolves in response to a changing information environment, it will be crucial for us to maintain the broadest possible vision of the future of information. The debate about "whither librarianship in the 21st century" is taking place concurrently with a far-reaching economic debate—"whither publishing?" Each of the following speakers will deal with subject matter that could be, and has, individually been the basis for separate conferences. While each of these subjects is of major interest for all of us, the sum comprises the basis for defining our current status in our countdown to the twenty-first century. If we are able to recognize that no technology of the past or the foreseeable future is important enough to become the sole driving force of information science and, instead, accept the premise that they all must coexist to provide our recipe for success, we will have succeeded in avoiding the current simplistic premise of the day, whatever the date. I know of no technological format that has replaced another format. I know of many that have the potential to do so, but the costs of conversion and the barrier of copyright have always forced us to continue to maintain the old *and* embrace the new. Even if conversion costs were not an issue, copyright has been the most formidable barrier of all. As technology makes it easier to achieve some sort of effortless conversion, the issue of intellectual property and the militancy of some publishers, or information entrepreneurs, as I now call the larger enterprise, has grown almost proportionately. If you think the twenty-first century holds uncertainty for us, imagine the fears of this important component of the scholarly communications partnership whose fears are based on the ambiguity of their future market. How do they get a fair return for a product that is so easily shared? I know, I know, the Xerox copier was ubiquitous when the 1976 Copyright Law was passed, but the new "Great Unknown" and the potential for the not-so clear-cut, documentable violations cause their paranoia. Pricing and relationships among publishers, libraries, and scholars should be based on a need to encourage the exchange of creativity. I believe that is what Mr. Jefferson and his friends had in mind when they were doing their creative thinking and acting a couple of centuries ago. In any case, the library will need to improve collections and services across technologies during the next decade. Realistic library directors and managers will maintain a broad and inclusive vision of the information horizon.

My final topic is politely termed "advocacy." In other words, the getting of money. Despite the high level of thinking that went into organizing this conference, the program does not touch upon this one significant element that I must lay claim to–that is, the high tariff for taking on the agenda that I have suggested to you. Information has always been an expensive commodity and is even more so today. It wasn't cheap when monks copied books by hand, even at their wages! Gutenberg dropped the unit cost briefly, but prices have been climbing ever since. The price for all of these splendid ideas is far more than any Provost would countenance at first blush. What are we to do?

The answer must come from the University Librarian. Generally speaking, the academic library of this era is run on a consultative basis. While a successful library director will stimulate creative thinking and discussions among the library's staff and constituents, he or she must ultimately make the final decisions and, more significantly, use the rhetoric and the substance of the discussions in packaging and selling the *range,* underline range, of products. Selling means raising the money necessary to provide the mix of products, services, staff and technology that is most sellable at that time, in that institution. There are three fundamental pies for the director to lust for in this endeavor: the institutional recurring budget, program improvement budgets which might or might not be recurring, and external funding (that is, grants, gifts, endowments, etc.). The director must use the rhetoric and substance at his/her command to craft a creative advocacy campaign. Not only will such advocacy generate resources, but it also can and should be used in defining the domain of the Library in the highly competitive campus environment.

To sum up: In recent years it has been *de rigueur* to say that the industrial age has ended and that the information age is upon us. Music to a librarian's ears! However, while it doesn't always feel like these words are entirely true, I believe that at this point the battle is close to being won, by and large. What I've been trying to posit is that librarians have steadily built collections and services employing the technology of each successive moment and maintaining each of these elements of service. Time and again, we have demonstrated that we have the right to the assignment by meeting and exceeding our constituents' expectations. The substance of our component services, our consortia, our advocacy, our technology, our mix of offerings, the character of our skills, and the scope of our facilities must all add up to the best possible response to the scholarly needs of our students, faculty and citizens. However, we've still got five years of work to do (and as I said earlier, we've probably got 10 years' work to do in five!) to meet the political, economic and professional challenges I've outlined today. If we are successful, we will have completed a strong platform from which to launch libraries into the 21st century. Our energy and creativity should fuel the fires of scholarship in 2011 just as they did in 1956. I look forward to hearing from the following speakers. They will define specific, programmatic challenges for us, as well as provide us with the next set of questions and possible answers allowing us to continue our professional evolution. I know that professionals of all eras think theirs has been the most monumental, but you'll be hard-pressed to find a twenty-five or thirty year span that has been as eventful as this one has been for our profession. I don't know when it was last possible to call the campus the ivory tower, implying a slow thoughtful pace. I have never seen it; at least I can't remember it! Thank you.

Collection Development in the Access Age: All You Thought It Would Be and More!

Connie Kearns McCarthy

We are coming to the end of the culture of the book. Books are still produced and read in prodigious numbers, and they will continue to be as far into the future as one can imagine. However, they do not command the center of the cultural stage. Modern culture is taking shapes that are more various and more complicated than the book-centered culture it is succeeding.[1]

Another one of "those" predictions, right? What caught my eye is that this is a quotation from the late O. B. Hardison, who was director of the Folger Shakespeare Library when I worked there early in my career. And certainly the Folger Library is a guardian of the culture of the book. What I think is particularly relevant for our discussion is the last sentence. "Modern culture is taking shapes that are more various and more complicated than the book-centered culture it is succeeding." I see bibliographers being directly engaged in making meaning of that complicated culture. The culture of collection development is also taking a different shape and we will have to do things differently to move to that new culture.

The collection development world has evolved dramatically in

Connie Kearns McCarthy is Associate University Librarian at Duke University Libraries in Durham, NC.

[Haworth co-indexing entry note]: "Collection Development in the Access Age: All You Thought It Would Be and More!" McCarthy, Connie Kearns. Co-published simultaneously in *Journal of Library Administration* (The Haworth Press, Inc.) Vol. 22, No. 4, 1996, pp. 15-31; and: *Access, Resource Sharing and Collection Development* (ed: Sul H. Lee) The Haworth Press, Inc., 1996, pp. 15-31. Single or multiple copies of this article are available from The Haworth Document Delivery Service [1-800-342-9678, 9:00 a.m. - 5:00 p.m. (EST). E-mail address: getinfo@haworth.com].

the past five years. At first I was tempted to say in the last decade, but if you think back on what library/collection development life was like in 1985–there is hardly any comparison to the issues and challenges we face today. The stage has been set and the many issues and challenges we discuss over the next two days are not new to any of us. What I would like to do is to take the perspective of how the current and possible future climate encourages, no, demands that we take a different approach to how we conduct our business of collection development. I will examine some of the broader trends, but also take a look from an institutional specific perspective.

I will first look at the current context by scanning the environment; secondly I will highlight the shifts in collection resources, follow that by looking at the bibliographer's role in this world, and finally look at how we move to the next world.

ENVIRONMENTAL SCAN OF THE ACCESS AGE

Let's look first at some of the issues that characterize our current environment for collection development. I identify the critical issues as: the access vs. ownership debate, restricted resource budgets, changing management strategies to maximize those budgets, and the impact of information technology. Articles abound on the access vs. ownership debate. While I acknowledge that ownership or access decisions are made on the micro level, I have never been comfortable with engaging the adversarial debate. We are looking at a broad collection philosophy of access and ownership that is here to stay. We have made those decisions in the past in a print-based environment as we have considered various resource sharing arrangements.

However, the costs of information access and delivery and the competition for collection dollars has taken the debate to a new level. The operational phrase at Duke University for the FY 95/96 budget is "growth by substitution." And yet we all know that when we face decisions of access and ownership, the substitutions are not equal, certainly not often in terms of cost, and that is without factoring in the need for the computer infrastructure support essential for electronic access. The issue of access is also larger than the library. The library is only an electronically viable operation if the university has the means to deliver.

Just as the library computing infrastructure is part of the larger system, so too are the resource budgets. The current political environment and the pressures on higher education budgets put us in competition for dollars. Resource budgets for the future will, at best, grow at modest rates. We feel the competition for those dollars as the information possibilities expand and it seems, that our users want everything. The challenges also present some opportunities for us to engage the political process and make some hard decisions. What collection assessment data do we have available? How does this mesh with the university data on support for the various academic programs? This is a process that is not always easy to engage, particularly since it means saying "no" or "less" to support of some programs and collections. But until we do that, we are not in a position to capitalize on the resource budget.

What are some of the ways that libraries are dealing with multiple demands and flat budgets? A variety of management strategies have emerged in the '90s for coping with flat resource budgets as identified in a survey of ARL libraries.[2] Most familiar are the consolidation or elimination of departments or positions, reduction of the number of managers as the organization is "flattened" with fewer supervisors or layers; cutting acquisitions budgets across the board, and a greater reliance on the importance of seeking external funding.

Not only are departments being merged or consolidated, but functions such as cataloging are being evaluated for possible outsourcing–taking greater advantage of vendor services for gains of efficiency and cost. Outsourcing is not a new strategy for libraries. We have dealt with contract services for many of our operations. Anyone familiar with government libraries knows that outsourcing has been a way of life for a long time. What is new in the current approach is that the "sacred cows,"–in-house cataloging, and title selection–are being evaluated for the process. I noted in the recent Stanford redesign document that item selection for trade and approval books is still in the process–but at the point that the books are shelf-ready. It will be interesting to see how practical that step is. I would venture to say that step is not needed, provided the profile is appropriate.

Staffing that is effective and efficient will continue to be a concern for academic libraries. Within the broader university context, we are beginning to see some slow movement on the part of administrators to downsize and in particular to examine the levels of hierarchy. With no growth budgets libraries have to carefully evaluate staff placement, levels of hierarchy in the organization and efficiency of staff positions. There comes a point where we will not be able to do more with less. We will indeed need to substitute, which means discontinuing some activities or positions. A Duke graduate student described growth by substitution as a lovely euphemism for killing one program to pay for growth in another.

Newer management strategies are beginning to be implemented in higher education and in academic libraries. Continuous Improvement (CI), or some elements of total quality management programs are gaining visibility. Much of the work in Continuous Improvement organizations is re-thinking and re-examining how we do our work; looking for better, more efficient ways to serve our customers. Along with this goes flattening the hierarchy and evaluating the role of senior administrators. This can be a challenging and healthy debate. It is a discussion that I have frequently with my colleagues at other institutions. The question "How do you flatten an AUL?" (an Assistant or Associate University Librarian) is real (but then that is the topic of another presentation I will give later in the month).

We cannot leave the environmental scan without addressing the rapid evolution of information technology and how it is profoundly changing our role as a provider of information resources. The changes are reflected in the vast array of information resources that are available, in the skills and competencies needed for our staffs, especially bibliographers, in the continuing training we must provide, in the budgeting for information resources, and in evaluating resource sharing opportunities. How do we build the agenda of strategic initiatives that take into account this changing environment?

Let me use this as an opportunity to talk about a process that the Duke Libraries used at the end of January to develop a library strategic plan and how that process pushed the agenda of hard choices. It will not only serve to illustrate the emphasis shared by staff on making those choices, but it also serves to illustrate that from an organizational perspective, we need to work in different ways. January 19-20 we gathered approximately 25% of the library staff (57), including staff from our Medical, Law, and business libraries, the CEO and a Vice President from one of our major jobbers, an administrator from our regional utility, the chair of our Library Advisory Board, a graduate student and a faculty member. The staff represented were from all working levels and areas of the library. At one of the sessions a panel of faculty talked about their needs from the library, where they want us to go. We are all aware of the various needs expressed by our users. The needs ranged from of course the very basic–I want to be able to find and retrieve the books I need or, I want the computer to work when I access it from off-site; to the idea from a physics faculty member to scan all our books. A graduate student in history acknowledged the need for the library to act as a clearinghouse for electronic information, but wanted to emphasize the traditional role of the library as an archive for primary and secondary materials.

Throughout the two days there were certain themes and tradeoffs that emerged. Customer focus was a dominant theme, but maybe not so surprising since we have been engaged in a continuous improvement program at Perkins Library for the past two years with a major emphasis on customer focus. Not a new concept you say, libraries and bibliographers, in particular, have always been focused on the customer. This is true, but I would venture to say that from the collection development perspective, we have focused on the individual needs of faculty, students and departments that the bibliographer serves. In the broader context, to have a customer focus for the library means that the customer feedback is an ongoing part of the management process in shaping our policies, procedures, and communications.

Let's leave this brief environmental scan for the moment, but keep in mind that the bibliographer is ideally placed conceptually to address these challenges. I have only identified a handful of issues: evaluating access and ownership, managing restrained resource budgets, an emphasis on the customer, changing management strategies, and responding to the multiple demands of the customers.

SHIFT IN COLLECTION RESOURCES

Let's now look at the shifting collection resources.

One of the factors that is changing the nature of research collections is the availability of a vast array of information resources. This wealth of resources has placed greater burdens on faculty, students and libraries. The reality is that libraries must provide easy and effective access to information and materials that the institution owns and to those that are available in the global information world. The information world and we librarians bombard the customer with a plethora of resources. The student and scholar face an increasing number of choices as they enter our online catalogs. In addition, they are apt to find individual access stations for additional resources located throughout the library. At Duke the choices include the Duke catalog, catalogs of our TRLN partners, North Carolina State University and University of North Carolina at Chapel Hill; about twenty five titles from a networked CD ROM tower, and on line databases through our catalog gateway. We at Duke have not yet reached that "seamless interface" Nirvana that we desperately seek. We're working on it.

It also seems that each class of students and each wave of young faculty comes a bit more computer literate and computer demanding than the last. And yet I was recently reminded that the information and the choices can be both confusing and overwhelming. I gave a list of books to retrieve from the stacks to my student assistant, a second semester freshman. There were about ten monograph titles to locate in the catalog, and retrieve from the stacks. The results of her search indicated that she did not have a clue about where to start. She got into Business Index and found a couple of book reviews, but never identified the titles in the online catalog.

Not only can the wealth of information be overwhelming, but more and more we exist in a global world and the "internationalization" of education, research and publishing is becoming a dominant theme in higher education. There is a growth in research publishing by non-European, non-western authors, and subsequently an increase in foreign publishing. The AAU/ARL Task Force on The Acquisitions and Distribution of Foreign Language and Area Studies Materials points out that this expansion is happening in a climate of decreasing acquisitions budgets and often a cutting back of the purchase of foreign publications. The task force looked at the gap between demand and availability for specialized materials. The task force offered recommendations based on the assumption that digitized information affords us some expanded opportunities that have not been available before now.

One of the conclusions of the task force was that in order to move to "a fully linked digitized network of research library collections, fundamental changes are needed to facilitate such a move. . . ." Foremost is the reallocation of acquisitions funds away from those "associated with building a self-sufficient collection" and toward "those associated with cooperative collection development and sharing." [3]

In moving to take advantage of these opportunities, the concept of cooperative collection development and resource sharing is essential and takes on new meaning. Resource sharing responsibilities in the new environment take on not only the activities of selecting, acquiring, cataloging, and providing bibliographic access, but also the responsibilities of preserving, archiving, and providing access in a digital format.

We need to re-evaluate resource sharing agreements that may have been made on a regional basis to achieve a level of comprehensiveness. The reality may have shifted and relationships need to be expanded and viewed from a broader perspective. The view for collections for the future becomes much more distributed. We, of course, need to balance more distributed needs for researchers and faculty with that of providing appropriate collection needs for undergraduates. What may well distinguish the research libraries of the future will not be how many volumes they hold (or how complicated they are to use!), but their in-depth collections in selected research fields, their ability to provide network access to those resources, and the library's agility in providing wide access to remote resources.

With the development of Internet tools, World Wide Web access, and online multimedia capabilities, the ability to take a whole discipline approach to resources will become a reality. The whole discipline approach takes the view that the scholar's need is access to collections regardless of format of materials or where they reside.

The approach is comprehensive–a composite of a number of individual collections composed of a variety of formats; published, text, manuscript, visual, and archival; organized around a theme, a culture, or a discipline.

In this environment a number of hard choices emerge. If full text is available online or from another resource sharing partner, how does this affect a decision to purchase and retain backfiles for the research collection? For the full text products that our undergraduates love–do we keep a current subscription and backfiles? Can the various research needs be met by online resources and document delivery firms? What if the document delivery firm only covers the articles in a journal and not the book reviews?

The evolution of our approaches to managing information can be characterized in three phases. Here I borrow liberally from the AAU/ARL Task Force on a National Strategy for Managing Scientific and Technological Information. The Task Force proposed three models to describe the various systems of scientific and scholarly communication. Other disciplines behave slightly differently, but the patterns are similar. I apply these models to characterize the shift in collection development approaches as well as the shift in collection costs from building tangible collections to the costs of data transfer with nothing tangible retained by the library. The models are classical, modernized, and emergent.[4] (See Figure 1.)

There are a number of implications for our collections and the role of the bibliographer if we look at the modernized and the emergent models. A critical element is that the supporting computer infrastructure is increasingly important. University and library funding for the information infrastructure is essential. As we move from local to remote sources, from a simple access structure to a very complex access structure, it becomes all too obvious very quickly if the access system does not perform adequately.

The complexity of the issue of electronic resources requires that the university and the library recognize the importance of funding for the information infrastructure. Ten years ago successful collection decisions would have meant that a title was identified, searched in the library's holdings, ordered, received and cataloged for the collection. Success in providing access in the diverse electronic environment means not only all of the above but choosing, funding,

FIGURE 1. Approaches to Managing Information

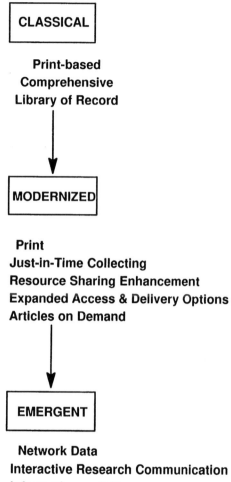

managing and providing system stability for access. And we all have our less than perfect scenarios.

I'd like to provide an institution-specific example of an experience in the shift to electronic access, an example of movement from the classical to the modernized model. In January 1993 I charged an electronic access committee with the task of moving more aggressively into providing electronic access. Our mandate was to take the serials inflationary increase for the 93/94 fiscal year ($358,000) and use those funds to make the shift. The guiding principle was that the funds were not to be spent on paper. The committee, as charged, had the responsibility, authority and resources to make the decisions for implementation by July 1. The committee, composed of bibliographers from the sciences, social sciences and humanities, the Head of the Collection Development department, and the Head of the Acquisitions/Serials department, were joined by library systems staff. They developed multiple strategies for access: cancellation of print sources; access to online sources through our catalog gateway, through direct access, providing CD-ROM titles through a networked tower, and subsidizing document delivery.

In using this example, my main purpose is to point out the changing role of the bibliographer in evaluating resources and making selection decisions and to use this as a case study in evaluating how we change the approaches to work in a team environment. First let's look at the benefits gained from the team approach. This committee was successful in achieving its goals and redirecting the funds to move electronic access from 4% of our materials budget to 16% for FY 93/94. As we evaluated teamwork overall in the last couple of years in a program of continuous improvement, we can identify several factors that supported the success of this team.

I draw on a definition of a team from Kaltzenbach, *The Wisdom of Teams*. A team is a "small number of people with complementary skills who are committed to a common purpose, have performance goals, and an approach for which they hold themselves mutually accountable . . . there are specific results for which the team is collectively responsible."[5] The struggle, or the area where the team felt less successful was their inability to guarantee the stability and support of the computing infrastructure necessary for delivery.

ROLE OF THE BIBLIOGRAPHER

Now I'd like to set the stage for rethinking the role of the bibliographer in this access age. To do that I'll use a vision of the academic library in 2010 developed by two of my colleagues at Duke, Ken

Berger and Rich Hines. This scenario informed discussions of the Rethinking Reference Institute held at Duke in June 1993.

The Academic Library in 2010

1. Users seldom come into the library building; if they do, it will be for:
- assistance with special problems
- casual/recreational reading (primarily in paper format)
- access to special equipment
- access for those who lack appropriate equipment and/or expertise
- contact with people
- study hall
- functions (e.g., wine and cheese parties)
- instruction, group and individual (though some will be done via remote access or off-site visits)

2. Nearly all serials will appear in digitized format (all will probably be produced using computer technology)

3. A high percentage of monographs will appear in digitized form, though much casual/recreational reading will still appear in paper format

4. Networking (the) standard
- remote electronic access to a wide variety of formats and information through networks will be the norm; the market will force a high degree of standardization

5. CD-ROMS will have passed away as networking provides the primary distributed access to large databases and text files
- CD-ROMS may have a niche as access to information for who may need a portable information resource (who may customize disks for specific needs while not able to access networks)

6. Full text retrieval will be at least as standard as retrieval of bibliographic information is today

7. Library staffing way down as labor intensive aspects of the library institution decrease

8. Front end systems for accessing databases will be much more intuitive, greatly reducing the need for information intermediaries

9. Individual access to high quality computer equipment–screens which facilitate easy reading and the use of varied media–a given for every member of the university community
10. Library acquisition, personnel and maintenance costs way down
11. Library out of direct charge loop for access to databases and information services
   - users will have their own accounts
   - university/library will serve as brokers to obtain special rates with information services
12. Library and librarians will serve gateway role and as facilitators to those who need special assistance and/or access to esoteric materials
13. Library will continue to serve as an archive/museum for special materials (e.g., manuscripts, rare books, primary source items)
14. Memory/storage capabilities dramatically up; costs equally reduced
15. Large percentage of library holdings converted to digitized form
16. Advanced technologies and techniques (e.g., cluster and vector analysis) are used to index materials, providing the capability to search efficiently and successfully though the large databases which will be available
17. There will be new licensing and use fee structures, which will be reflective of the larger user base and lower-cost per use
   - assessments will be more directly tied to the information user[6]

What are the implications of this vision for rethinking collection development and in particular, rethinking the role of the bibliographer?

First of all, perhaps we should begin the rethinking with the term bibliographer. "Resource manager," or "resource specialist." might be a better term that encompasses a broader definition than what is defined in the dictionary as "one versed in the description and cataloging of printed matter, one who compiles a bibliography."[7]

We will continue to need resource specialists for our research libraries, particularly in the area of specialized language and area studies. These librarians will need to be multi-talented. The economic reality will continue to have an effect on our staffing for collection development and we will employ cross-functional staff. The areas of specialty become broader, the specialist will work in a team environment. Perhaps the East Asia specialist is part of a processing team that is responsible for any special cataloging and index needs in that language. And also part of a public services team that provides specialized instruction in Internet resources. Rather than focusing narrowly on academic departments or programs, resource specialists need to be grouped by disciplines, with a broad view across departments, and with the ability to work with interdisciplinary programs and resources.

In many ways the activities of a current bibliographer remain the same but the changing environment provides the opportunity for a greater use of skills and expertise. What will be the work of this re-defined bibliographer?

- collection development, evaluation, selection, and management of resources; local, networked and remote
- decision-making regarding resource-sharing commitments
- development of strategies and software for subject/discipline network access
- management of financial resources to meet collection, access, and resource-sharing needs
- providing specialized research assistance to users, networked or local
- informing and assisting users in the use of databases and electronic resources
- creation of specialized databases
- development and fund raising; participation with faculty in fund-raising efforts, grant applications.

To guide the evaluation and selection of resources, the librarian needs to develop a resource map. Dan Hazen, in a recent article, urged that we think of a collection policy as a hypertext information map.[8] As we develop our Duke Library web page, I see this information map played out on a web page to guide the user to the multitude of sources, including a hot link to the resource specialist. (See Figures 2 and 3.)

Perhaps the web page had an earlier incarnation and there was

FIGURE 2

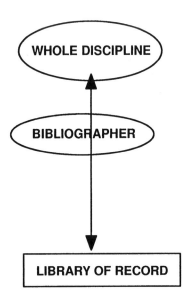

FIGURE 3

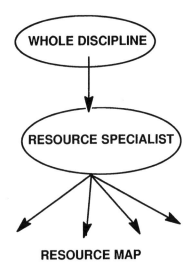

always a role for the guide through the maze. The resource specialist becomes a "make of meaning," the guide through the labyrinth.

Let's sketch out our own scenario for collection development in 2010.

COLLECTION DEVELOPMENT IN 2010

1. Organization/structure
- Resource specialists organized by disciplines; social sciences, sciences, humanities, interdisciplinary studies, international area studies
- Shared consortial language/area specialists
- Specialists serve on self-managed teams; responsible for acquiring, licensing, processing, public services within team
- Coordination/decisions for CD program carried out by cross-functional teams: no AUL for CD

2. Budgeting
- Self managed resource budget team with responsibility for all resource budget decisions. A member of the team serves on the library leadership team.
- Budgets are coordinated with library and campus computing needs. Flexible funding allows specialist to purchase computing infrastructure needs.

3. Collection Policies
- Dynamic policies or resource map available on WWW with links to new local sources, resource specialist
- Web links to local and networked resources; primary, multimedia resources

4. Skills/competencies needed for resource specialists
- Highly developed skills in information retrieval
- Ability to work and assume responsibilities in a team based environment
- Skill in analyzing, leveraging, and maximizing scarce budget resources
- Collaborative communication skills in soliciting and responding to user feedback

- Ability to view discipline resource needs at a conceptual level–to anticipate user needs, to create and build resource maps

And now a step further, a "day in the life" of a Humanities resource specialist at Duke University in 2010.

The humanities resource specialist has a background in art history, with language specialties of French and German. She is based in our Lilly Library which houses the collections for Art, Art History, Dance, Drama, Philosophy and the media collection. This library was recently expanded to include the music and music media collection which was previously in a separate building on the same campus.

Some of the activities for the day include:

- Making decisions on resource expenditures for external grant funds; beginning to think of an approach to take in applying to resource budget team for in-house grant funds
- Writing up the collection and access assessment for the Women's Studies program review
- Checking library database to review recent humanities and particularly art materials arrivals through PromptCat
- Checking library database to see what titles need her cataloging attention–2 titles in Japanese will need consultation with the East Asian specialist.
- 2:00-4:00–Serve at the Assist desk in Lilly Library. Help a freshman begin a search for an article; talk to an art faculty member and ask if she has seen the new art files web page from . . . ; answer a call from a faculty member at home who is having problems accessing the Duke data bank (tries her known tricks, will have to consult with the systems person on the Humanities team)
- Spend some time evaluating new products, evaluating license agreement, developing list of questions to ask purchasing agent
- Plan issue identifier for Humanities team meeting; problems have cropped up with tracking and shelving print and accompanying media materials. Some things don't change! I thought we had solved this one years ago!

How do we move to the academic library in 2010? I have avoided using the "p" word up to now. We do need a new paradigm for the research library and for collection development in particular. We have not even begun to "re-think" collection development as we have begun to examine other areas of our profession. But rather than a new paradigm I offer a new perspective, that of the crystal pyramid. We no longer have the luxury of using a crystal ball. The perspective is anything but smooth. There are sharp angles, many perspectives, and several choices of direction that are sharp and jagged. There are risks involved in making some of those choices.

As I review the titles of the presentations for this conference, I see another variation of a future search conference. We are indeed searching for new and different strategies for access, resource sharing and collection development. There are no easy solutions. We are creating new models and experimenting with different strategies.

In conclusion, I'd like to leave you with a short pithy remark offered by one of our faculty members from our future search conference. I suspect that it will lead nicely into the following presentations. He encouraged the Duke Library staff to "Seek persistent disequilibrium." I encourage all of us to gaze into our crystal pyramids, make the risky choices, and seek persistent disequilibrium.

NOTES

1. O. B. Hardison, Jr., *Disappearing Through the Skylight: Culture and Technology in the Twentieth Century.* (New York: Viking, 1989), p. 264.

2. *Resource Strategies in the 90s: Trends in ARL University Libraries.* Washington, DC: Association of Research Libraries. 1994, pp. 15-20.

3. *Reports of the AAU Task Forces on Acquisitions and Distribution of Foreign Language and Area Studies Materials, A National Strategy for Managing Scientific and Technological Information, Intellectual Property Rights in an Electronic Environment.* Washington, DC: Association of Research Libraries, p. 11.

4. *Reports of the AAU Task Forces,* pp. 58-61.

5. Jon R. Katzenbach and Douglas K. Smith, *The Wisdom of Teams: Creating the High-Performance Organization.* (Boston: Harvard Business School Press, 1993), p. 45.

6. Ken Berger and Rich Hines. *The Academic Library of the Future: A Year 2010 Draft Plan for the Duke University Libraries.* Internal document. February, 1992.

7. *The American Heritage Dictionary of the English Language.* (Boston: Houghton Mifflin, 1971), p. 129

8. Dan C. Hazen, "Collection Development Policies in the Information Age," *College and Research Libraries* 56 (January 1995): 30.

Redesigning Research Libraries:
First Step Toward the 21st Century

Charles A. Hamaker

Occasionally in library literature, someone writes something that you wish you had written. In a recent issue of *College and Research Libraries* Dan C. Hazen of Harvard College Library has given me the pleasure of seeing in someone else's words something I've thought for years, but never had complete enough insight to say. His article "Collection Development Policies in the Information Age" claims that collection development policies " . . . are exercises in obsolescence that cater to nostalgic longing for order, precision and prescription."[1] They are described in the article as "monuments of defensiveness" and "enshrinements of obsolescence" or when they are accurate as "codifications of decline." His point is that the "stream of new materials" that selectors grapple with "increasingly cross(es) traditional boundaries of format and discipline." He is absolutely correct.

How does an individual selector, who may well have had a hand in deciding to use CARL UnCover as a source for journal articles, describe that resource in a traditional conspectus approach to collections? It is not "owned" per se, does not fit just "one" subject area, may well be funded from various sources, and in sum doesn't fit in a traditional collection development policy statement.

Charles A. Hamaker is Assistant Dean for Collection Development at Louisiana State University Libraries in Baton Rouge, LA.

[Haworth co-indexing entry note]: "Redesigning Research Libraries: First Step Toward the 21st Century." Hamaker, Charles A. Co-published simultaneously in *Journal of Library Administration* (The Haworth Press, Inc.) Vol. 22, No. 4, 1996, pp. 33-48; and: *Access, Resource Sharing and Collection Development* (ed: Sul H. Lee) The Haworth Press, Inc., 1996, pp. 33-48. Single or multiple copies of this article are available from The Haworth Document Delivery Service [1-800-342-9678, 9:00 a.m. - 5:00 p.m. (EST). E-mail address: getinfo@haworth.com].

33

Yet, it is an important resource for the kind of cross-disciplinary research that goes on in our institutions. It is a basic resource for keeping current on the major journals of a given field with its new Reveal (TM) function, and any bibliographer who didn't mention it to a faculty member or even graduate student in a rapidly develop-ing field where the library was unable to keep up with the new journals, would be failing in her basic responsibilities of providing information resources for research and teaching. Hazen's answer to this problem is a new type of statement that describes all formats of information and resources both local and remote in each of the fields the library accepts responsibility. This in effect is a roadmap of information which would take the place of the traditional collec-tion development statement.

I'm not sure of his answer, but I am positive that his question is right. It is time for a critical reexamination of the role and form of the collection development policy. But there are several other "areas" of information that I think need to be incorporated into such a document, other indicators that should guide collection decisions and be included in policy statements. I have a specific example of why we should incorporate large scale resources like UnCover into the local collection development policy. At LSU, we have a Center for Coastal Studies and an Oceanographic Institute. UnCover has just announced that the Woods Hole Oceanographic Institute will start adding its titles and tables of contents to the database this spring. Wouldn't it be a disservice not to mention that resource in the policy that covers those areas for LSU?

I don't know what final form a collection development policy in this new age should take, but I know that major challenges to traditional assumptions in collection management are just beginning for academic libraries.

They are not *just* the result of new technologies, new means of accessing, storing, purchasing and leasing information. Those are significant issues and library literature is replete with the arguments going on over those new formats. But that is not the reason I see libraries stepping into an arena of rapid change. There are severe problems in funding that have become endemic to academic libraries, and will continue to plague us for the next decade and on into the next century, but that is not the primary challenge for collection development in academic libraries.

No, the primary driver, the primary motivator for changes in academic libraries as we enter the next century will not be technology, will not be funding. It will be change in the Academy and its response to the outside world. Change in missions, and in goals and in basic understandings of the nature and utility of information, will be the fundamental forces behind change in libraries.

Consider this. There are some verities that we have lived by in academic libraries. We have taken on collection goals based in part on attempting to correlate the local mission of our university with the universe of publications. And our collection development policies, the formal descriptions of what we do and why we do it have been in terms of the level of coverage of a specific literature or literatures related to those broader institutional goals. Thus, if we have a significant institutional investment in Tibetan art, its study and research, in collections, grants, and teaching programs, we have taken that institutional investment to signal a library collection goal that may mean a level "4" or even "5" in conspectus terms. What if that program in Tibetan art loses grant funding, loses students, but still has a degree program and some faculty in place, though they are not replaced as they leave? At the same time, without any additional funding for the library, a new program comes into existence in Chinese cave paintings. There is a groundswell in student involvement in terms of credit hours. There are new courses, or perhaps a renumbering or relabeling of older courses. Graduate students flock to the university for this exceptional program. What happens to Tibetan art in the meantime? Under the model we have generally followed, it continues (because of historical antecedents) to be a collecting goal, and we simply "add" Chinese cave painting. Remember I specified no new resources. Is it reasonable to assume we will just "add" a new area with flat resources?

Of course not, but we do it every working day. In part we have been lulled by our environment. Our institutions have been loathe to state that Tibetan art is no longer a priority for fear of offending a constituency. But the demands for Chinese cave paintings will be real. In the beginning, the faculty may be content to use their own resources and provide them for the students as well. In fact, we may have never been advised by the university that there is such a new program in existence. It may be buried in the Curriculum and Instruction Committees' work with new course development. But sooner or later, students will come to us expecting resources. Faculty, probably new or perhaps reassigned from other areas, will want support. When do we know this has happened? Is it when professor X asks for help? Or are their other ways that we can recognize those needs, validate them and respond to them? What do we do? On paper, in our written policies, we probably accommodate both programs. In reality, we probably start shirking one subject for the other.

Where can we find the clearest proof that such a shift is necessary? How do we defend the shift? I know just such types of programmatic shifts are occurring throughout academia right now. The institution is responding to the broader world, often without acknowledgement of the new programs, often without "new" resource assignment, often without notifying library or in some cases even the administration, that such a shift is occurring or is in the works. The earliest warning signs of such shifts and the most defensible data that we can use are readily at hand in our own OPACS and internal university documentation long before there is any possibility of official action, official "restructuring," official "re-engineering," or official prioritization.

As a collection development librarian I have been lulled into a false sense of security by some excellent research that has been reported over the last decade. The most significant research suggests that inputs drive circulation. The more you spend, up to a certain level, the more circulation you get. Concomitant with that has been the work by Paul Metz at VPI, Virginia Polytechnic Institute and State University, in his monumental circulation study *The Landscapes of Literature* and in the 1982 and 1987 studies of circulation at VPI. He reported in the article "Measuring Collections Use at Virginia Tech" that comparing circulation from 1982 with 1987 showed that "Circulation statistics are extraordinarily stable over time and extraordinarily insensitive to minor differences in measurement techniques."

He compared a two day snapshot of circulation in 1982 with a month's circulation in 1987. He found that circulation transactions across 29 subject categories for the months of January through May of 1987 were essentially interchangeable. There were no significant variations in subject patterns throughout the academic year. He also found that comparing 1982 circulations with 1987 circulations revealed very high correlation coefficients. That is, there is an "extraordinary measure of stability, indicating that circulation patterns in an institution not undergoing dramatic curricular change or extensive changes in the direction of library acquisitions are remarkably constant . . . a single measure of circulation use drawn at any normal time in a given school year may provide an academic library with measures on which it can rely for a considerable period of time."[2]

One rule of life in this new age is test your assumptions. And in the routine business of making sure our assumptions were still OK, we were able to compare circulation from 1987-89 at LSU with our circulation in 1993-94. Once again, we were looking, as Metz had, at about a half decade. He had done it and discovered no change. When we looked we found that there was measurable change in our circulation patterns. On even the most obvious scale, which subjects ranked highest in circulation, there were changes. On a more detailed examination we found that who checked out which books had also changed. I take some comfort in not knowing this before from something Terrence Brooks wrote in 1984. He indicated " . . . high levels of randomness in library-output statistics inhibit the performance of sophisticated forecasting methods." In other words, he said naive forecasting methods work best for figuring out the future. I am statistically naive. Brooks would be happy with me. These two statements, one from Metz, the other from Brooks, look disparate enough that they must not have been dealing with the same numbers. But all Brooks meant was that fancy regression methods don't do much good in forecasting circulation. On the ground level, Metz's assertion that what you see is what there is, and Brooks', that you can't do it with multiple regression, in fact are similar. But both approaches also tell us that you have to measure it to know what it is.

What has happened at LSU since 1987-89 to make our circulation by subject area unstable? And what does it mean for collection development? These are the big questions, and they are exactly where I think a policy needs to cover something other than what has traditionally been included. Circulation measures, especially in a changing environment, are critical to the best use of library resources. Here is a table that provides an overview of our primary patron categories, comparing the 1987-89 circulation patterns with 1993-94 and the fall 1988 primary patron groups with the fall of 1993. As you can see, there are significant changes in circulation patterns, and although the overall numbers of patrons are relatively unchanged, there are wider swings in particular areas.

Comparison of circulation and patron categories
LSU Libraries 1987-89 and 1993-94

	Faculty	Graduate	Undergrad.	Others
CIRCULATION				
1987-89	12.82%	32.91%	42.99%	8.33%
1993-94	10.70%	42.91%	34.36%	9.59%
ENROLLMENT				TOTALS
fall 1988	1277	4308	22256	27841
fall 1993	1291	5329	20040	26660

As you can see from this table, there was an overall decrease of less than 1200 in our primary patron categories. These numbers come from official university enrollment and faculty counts. From a macro level, and with the "security" of Metz's observations this doesn't look like a big change. But you will notice that there was a significant jump in graduate student enrollment, about a 20% increase overall, and a 10% decrease in undergraduate enrollment. What that produced was a change that is significant with regards to who our primary users of books are. In the earlier time period, undergraduates checked out more books than any other category of patron. In the more recent year, graduates became our single largest users of books.

There have not been a lot of new programs introduced at LSU in the past five years. But the university has increased enrollment standards, and clearly from these numbers, increased emphasis on graduate programs. Part of this is a side effect. In 1987 LSU became a Research I University, a status dependent on research dollars from the federal government. This has meant increased graduate student levels in many of our science and technology departments. The Research I status was a long term goal of the university. But the increased graduate student levels are in part a result of the process of increasing federal research dollars. And that, as the table shows, did not mean much of a decrease in overall enrollment, but at a significant jump in the graduate student load. In turn, that has impacted the mix of circulation emphasis we've seen in the library. All of this occurred without a "directive" or prioritization document from the university telling us to change our emphasis in selection. In some subject areas the change in use has been dramatic.

CHANGES IN CIRCULATION PATTERNS OF 20% OR MORE
1987/89 AND 1993/94
AREAS WITH 1000+ CIRCULATIONS

	1987-1989 PERCENT FACULTY& GRADS	1993-1994 PERCENT FACULTY & GRADS	CHANGE
HQ SEX ETC	33%	56%	23%
HV SOC WRK	28%	49%	22%
JK CONST.HIST	38%	58%	21%
ND PAINTING	29%	49%	20%
TD ENVIR. ENG	39%	66%	27%
TK ELEC ENG	41%	71%	30%
Z BIBL	51%	90%	39%

First of all, let me make clear what these percentages do not mean. They don't mean that graduates are more interested in sex now than they were 5 years ago! And they don't mean that undergraduates are less interested in sex either.

In the 1987-89 period our primary clientele for HQ titles was undergraduates (some 60% of the use at that time). Today 56% of HQ circulations are from graduates and faculty.

What has happened? Well yes, our MSW (Master of Social Work program) increased enrollment by 10%, but that is only 21 students. Our Ph.D. in Psychology increased by 23%, or about 26 students. The MA in Sociology program increased by a whopping 67%, but that only means they went from 9 graduate students to 16. And our Ph.D in Sociology increased from 20 candidates to 28, a 40% increase. In Sex, we are averaging over 7,500 circulations a year. Surely these small numbers of students couldn't account for this much of a shift. I seriously doubt that they did. What has changed significantly is the nature of research. Who is looking at the history of sex today? Not just curious undergrads.

Ever since Foucault, everyone is interested in the history of sex and sexual matters. That means that our French department and our English department and even yes, our History department are interested in approaches and issues now that were not of much concern five to seven years ago. There is almost a whole new industry sprung full grown in gender studies, gay and lesbian studies, the history of sexuality. And it is exploding on an inter-disciplinary level. I would guess that even in libraries where there has been no growth in institutional programs like social work and psychology and sociology the concentration of use in the HQ's has changed significantly over the last 5 years. I am suggesting of course, that it is *not* library acquisitions per se that have caused a change in dynamics, not even institutional change. We are not talking about new programs, which Metz suggests might cause shifts, but a dramatic change in the nature of research. Foucault is not just the province of curious undergrads and people with "professional" concerns in sex research. His work is central to how Academia, specifically the humanities, is re-interpreting every aspect of our culture. I repeat, it does not seem to me that this particular change is institution-specific. Rather, it is a reflection of trends in the larger academy. And back to Hazen again for a moment. As the context of subject areas mutates because of new emphases, the LC classification schedule seems less and less relevant to a "subject" specialist dealing with research trends. Today our English and American literature liaison has to know as much about the history of homosexuality as she does about Mark Twain or William Shakespeare!

Is there an institutional explanation for the jump in graduate and faculty interest in Constitutional History? In this category there are some fairly small numbers, as circulations go. I limited this list to areas with 1,000 or more circulations per year, but JK only averages about 1,300. There actually are student numbers behind this increase. The Political Science MA program more than doubled, from 9 to 22 students in the years covered and perhaps as important our Ph.D.'s in history jumped from 37 to 63. Painting is also an understandable increase. Between 1988 and 1993 our Art History MA program quadrupled. Environmental Engineering also saw a huge increase of graduate students, from 23 to 72. But Electrical Engineering, the TK's represent another case of the rest of the universe outpacing library classification schemes. Many computer techie books end up in TK and I don't need to explain to anyone how explosive the demand for this material is.

What I believe is happening in many of these areas is a combination of factors. Some growth in graduate programs is causing a shift in the demographics of use. But even more dramatic is the phenomena of forces outside the library, outside our purchasing decisions, outside even the local campus, impacting library usage. The larger issues of intellectual trends are moving use outside traditional boundaries. We are being forced out of narrow approaches in narrow subjects. We are being forced out of preconceptions about how our material is being used and by whom. We have to change what we think the bibliographer or selector's scope and role should be. And collection development, if it is to be relevant in this new world, and library collections, if they are to be relevant, are going to react to these external forces or become extraneous. Circulation tracking is just one means of identifying and then preparing to initiate changes in what we do and how we do it. Circulation studies and their analysis must become an integral part of ongoing collection policies. We must state explicitly that we will utilize circulation data, tracking such variables as the use population, changes over time, even departmental charges, to guide future purchasing decisions. LSU's data show over 49 LC class areas where there are changes of 10% or more in patron use categories, and 21 LC Class areas where the change is 15% or larger. This is not a small change. It is off the scale of our expectations, off the scale of our experience.

Libraries have been bastions of quietude, islands of solace, contemplative towers. And too often some academic librarians have taken on the characteristics of those who are least responsive to change. We have seen change, and will see even more in technical services. Our literature tells us this. But this talk should be a wake up call to collection managers, to bibliographers, to selectors and liaisons. We are in the midst of a major sea change, even in the area we thought we knew best: the books we add to our libraries. Use patterns are unstable, after perhaps decades of stability. And that means who we are buying for is changing dramatically.

A major key to the future is defining our user base, our customer base. And as we migrate to electronic tools, that must continue to be a major concern, and should be built into any output measurements we create. To get the resources to support acquisition, no matter how we define that word, we have to know who we are supporting. Academic libraries have generally operated under a sort of umbrella that is nebulously described as for the good of library patrons. One of the things we should have learned from the outside world is market segmentation, identifying who our customers are. Glib easy answers are no longer applicable. It is not just the universe of students at our institutions, or the faculty, it is the larger forces at work in our changing environment defined in the largest context.

Who and what becomes a critical question when defending resource allocation in the future. We have thought it was sufficient to measure rates of increase in cost of various materials, then suggest what portion of the universe we needed to collect to defend budget figures. That is the past. The future is one of accountability and ability to adapt to changing user needs.

User needs are a major concern not only for books we buy, but for our serials collections as well. In fact most of us believe our serials collections serve rather immediate needs, especially the expensive sci-tech titles. As I reported at this conference last year, LSU is in the process of redesigning its serials collection. Our philosophy is simple. We have tried all the standard approaches for controlling a serials budget that now is almost 80% of our total materials budget.

We have been through two major cancellation reviews in the last few years, the most recent in 1992. That final cancellation yielded $650,000 in cuts. Our faculty participated in both reviews but I have to report that overall the effect on them of participating in the decision-making process was negative. They were negative exercises, emotional, frustrating. We learned from those two projects that sending lists of titles to departments to be marked or ranked resulted in identification and marking of titles that in fact were not necessarily of high priority. Faculty responded to perception of a title's importance, even if they did not know the title itself. Thus one of our science departments ranked *Sulphur* as important to research. Surely if there was a scientific journal in our libraries by that name it would be important. But in fact, *Sulfur* is a poetry journal.

The end result of marking of many lists was to reduce our subscription list, without attending to what was really needed, a redesign of our serials collection.

In talking with faculty we learned that there were critical titles we weren't subscribing to that they desperately needed. And there were other titles that, yes, they had marked as "save" but which were of much less importance. All of the effort in identifying cancellations did not lead to a single new subscription. The last time we had added new subscriptions was 1986. This was a situation that could not continue.

The Faculty Senate Library Committee and the administration of LSU Libraries sought a new approach that would allow the Libraries to cope with the budget situation. Clearly, in this environment, traditional solutions, the drop one or two to add one or two, would not work. We needed a radical redirection of our approach to serials. Philosophically we found that in recognizing that we could no longer attempt to collect broadly and deeply. However, 1.6 million dollars is a lot of money. We believed that kind of budget could buy what the faculty needed to support their teaching and research if we collected in a more focused manner.

Our solution was to identify what should be available locally and at the same time identify titles that were appropriate for access via document delivery. Criteria we developed and discussed included such concerns as whether there were halftone photos, symbols or graphs and charts that would not photocopy well, and most importantly, titles which were used often enough that ready and frequent in-house access was a necessity.

We conducted two pilot projects, which I reported on at this conference last year. Realizing that sending out lists led to easy marking of lots of titles rather than focused decision making, that providing lists pre-determined the faculty's selection, we approached Chemistry and later Geography /Anthropology as pilots to help us identify titles needed in-house for instructional and research activities and titles which could be safely accessed via document delivery.

The results were astounding. In 1989 our Chemistry department had identified 410 journals as important to teaching and research. But when we gave each faculty member a blank sheet of paper and asked each which titles were needed for their own research and teaching, they identified 287 titles. We own 74% of the titles they identified. However, they also told us that 18% of the titles we currently subscribe to were reasonable for document delivery. We learned that over one third of the titles we currently subscribe to were of interest to single faculty members. And 35 of the journals that we currently house in the Chemistry library were not listed by any faculty member. Twenty of those titles had been ranked as essential in previous rankings!

Geography/Anthropology had even more surprises in store for us. Their faculty had identified 1,808 journals in our 1989 ranking. In the 1993 pilot project they identified 535 journals as important to teaching and research. Of those 535 titles, we own 59%. For that department, 30% of the titles identified are candidates for document delivery.

As we did this pilot with these two departments, we introduced them to a table of contents/document delivery service, UnCover, and offered them and their graduate students free document delivery. As it became clear to us that we could afford their needs, we gradually have opened up this program to all of the departments on campus. Since we have now been using document delivery as an integral part of our libraries' effort to support teaching and research for over a year, we evaluated in detail the last six months of our orders for articles.

We ordered articles from 540 journals. Sixty of the journals we ordered articles from are titles we own, about 75 articles. This was generally because a particular issue had not arrived, was misshelved and couldn't be located, was missing an article or was at the bindery. In all we ordered 1006 articles for a total cost of $12,278.14. Of that total, $5,740 was for copyright fees. If we had subscriptions to the 480 journals we ordered articles from, they would have cost us, for 1994, $207,000. Because some of the orders were from multiple years of journals, our cost to acquire those titles would have been considerably higher than this because of backruns, binding, processing, shelving, cataloging and all the other processes we support for journals we receive.

Considering that we cancelled $650,000 in journals in 1992-93 we think we got a bargain. Our experience with service and delivery has been exceptional. Our complaints are typical. We wish UnCover would hurry up with getting more access, more portals, quicker response time, you know–the technical stuff.

In continuing our serials redesign project, we have assigned library liaisons to each of our departments, and for the science, engineering and agriculture departments, each liaison has met with the department, explained our project, taught them how to use UnCover and especially REVEAL. We have also requested their *individual* input into our serials redesign project. We have not had all of the participation we wanted, but I can report that an average of 50% of the faculty (slightly higher in some departments) has returned lists to us of titles identified for either hardcopy subscription or document delivery access.

As part of our ongoing evolution, we have developed a fairly careful system of guidelines for Inter Library Borrowing to use in determining when to go to a document delivery source. All requests for journal titles that have been cancelled or which have lapsed are searched and ordered via CARL UnCover for our patrons. If the title is not available from the CARL system, other document suppliers are used. I have to admit our success with other suppliers has not been as high as with UnCover. If any copyright fee exceeds $20.00 and we have not exceeded our copyright limitations for the year for so-called "free" articles, (i.e., fewer than five requests per title per year) the patron can choose to pay the overage for UnCover, or we will attempt to acquire the article from a supplier who might have a lower copyright fee (I'm sure Becky Lenzini is not happy to hear that this is sometimes possible). The patron may choose for us to obtain the article from one of our reciprocal borrowing partners, which usually means a much slower turnaround. We have had very few articles hit this $20.00 limit. Our average copyright fee is about $5.70. For titles we have never subscribed to, but where we are over the copyright limit of five, we will send requests to a commercial document supplier with the lowest cost, regardless of turnaround time.

For titles the library has never subscribed to, we normally go to a reciprocal library, or if we have ordered fewer than five times and the journal doesn't fall in any other category I've mentioned. We also use our borrowing partners for articles that are more than ten years old. We charge patrons if they want more than ten articles from the same journal in a year for volumes previous to 1993. They are expected to pay half the charge for each additional request over the ten copies per title limit. However, beginning with the 1994 year, because that is the year we agreed to accept the philosophy integrating document delivery with ownership, journals dated 1994 or later do not have a ten articles cutoff. For extremely heavy users of our services, we negotiate some cost sharing. This is particularly true when we know the individual has a grant which may defray some of the costs.

As you can see this is a very cautious approach. We are feeling our way into this document delivery/in-house ownership philosophy.

In our serials redesign project, the key to success is the personal relationship the library liaison builds with the department chair and through departmental meetings with the individual faculty. We routinely try to meet with the faculty in a room that at least has a telephone line, or other means for getting to UnCover so we can specifically demonstrate how it works, that it is not vaporware! We provide our personal e-mail addresses and phone numbers so they can contact our liaison if something doesn't work. And believe me, they do call. We have had a lot of compliments from the faculty over this approach.

It is not negative, holds the promise of real change, of a realistic assessment of their in-house needs, and of a service that actually delivers. They not only have a name, they have a face, a real person who is interested in meeting their information needs. This approach takes the user survey to what we believe is a new level. We no longer have anonymous faces or even "departmental" level information to rely on for determining our journal and serial needs. We know who wants what journals. One of the major journal users in the Geography/Anthropology department recently left LSU. In discussing this with the chair of the department, we learned that no, the department is not going to replace him with someone in the same areas of specialization, but is adding a faculty member with very different needs. We now have the mechanism, with this survey, not only to identify what the new faculty member needs, but to scrutinize the titles that support only that previous faculty member. This is a long distance from the collections based, "in depth" field coverage, collection as a conspectus number approach. It is targeted, and yet we believe it will help us meet the real and present and changing needs of one of the top research universities in the country.

I discussed the vague outlines of this collection approach several years ago with the Dean of the largest libraries on the continent. She said to me, doesn't this mean we are all headed for a kleenex approach in collections. I hadn't thought through the issues then, and am still in the process of doing so, but I can answer with an emphatic no.

It does mean we cannot be all things. It does mean in refocusing our collecting strategy, we can choose the areas where we will remain strong, deep and broad. Recently I chaired what we called internally, an access task force. Its mission was to come up with processing guidelines to help us control the literally millions of bibliographic units that are outside of our control at the moment. It was clear that hard choices were needed. The taskforce identified the core collections that constitute LSU's unique addition to the world of information, the archival center of our collections. I must admit they do not include things we would like to do, such as continue our fine small press poetry magazine focus, or our arctic research collections. But surviving intact, and I believe strengthened by the process, was our commitment to core collecting areas that have been our strengths for generations. Because they are logical for our locale, our state, our institutions, they will remain strengths for the foreseeable future. Those areas are not particularly narrow. We will continue our traditional focus on Louisiana and the lower Mississippi Valley. This is where our manuscript collections are strongest, and where our book and serial collections have always been superb. This also means that we will no longer spend our limited cataloging and processing resources on the ephemera of education, or international architecture, or the small poetry presses of the UK. But we are newly dedicated to focusing on *our* priorities: sugarcane and rice culture, even though the university no

longer has a sugarcane program, coastal processes, southern literature and a long list of other unique areas where our contribution to
the national and international "virtual" collection is needed. We
have not stopped in-depth collecting, we have refocused our energies, not only in collecting, but in cataloging, processing, and preservation. If you look out our efforts on the World Wide Web you
will see some current results of this focus. Yes, it spills over even
into our electronic efforts. I have colleagues at other larger universities who refer to the "great collections" concept as an ongoing
commitment. Louisiana has and will continue to have great collections. We will leave a legacy of focus, of energy, of direction for our
collections. But it will not be the omnibus collection of yesteryear,
where any slip of paper in a veritable cornucopia of subjects was
not only acquired, but processed, cataloged, bound, and serviced.

Tomorrow's research library will still be a research library. But it
will be a library with a clearer understanding of mission, of its
users, of its future and yes, of its past. It will not attempt more than
it can afford to do well, and continuously. As technical services all
over the country are being redesigned, research collections too will
be redesigned. If we stay aware of the currents that affect our
activities, if we stay committed to moving ahead in these amazing
times we not only will survive, we will prosper.

NOTES

1. Dan C. Hazen. "Collection Development Policies in the Information Age"
College and Research Libraries 56, 1 (January, 1995): 29-31.
2. Paul Metz and Charles A. Litchfield. "Measuring Collections Use at Virginia Tech." *College and Research Libraries* (November, 1988): 501-513.

Delivery of Documents and More:
A View of Trends Affecting Libraries and Publishers

Rebecca T. Lenzini

Isn't there an old adage which maintains that library science is the (next) oldest profession? That being the case, document delivery must be among the oldest services. After all, libraries have delivered documents to users since their creation; interlibrary loan is organized explicitly for document delivery between and among institutions.

"Document delivery" to our ears, however, has a more specific meaning. The term connotes a commercial or specialized approach to the delivery of information, whether the activity occurs in the public or private sector. While ILL is based by definition entirely on an institution's collection, document delivery implies the ability to reach beyond a single collection and to combine multiple resources in meeting a document request.

All of us attending this conference are aware of a number of trends affecting each of us in our various roles within the field of information. Given my own involvement in the area of document delivery, I would like to focus on four trends relating specifically to this area, its future, and its impact on both the publisher and the library.

Rebecca T. Lenzini is President of CARL Corporation in Denver, CO.

[Haworth co-indexing entry note]: "Delivery of Documents and More: A View of Trends Affecting Libraries and Publishers." Lenzini, Rebecca T. Co-published simultaneously in *Journal of Library Administration* (The Haworth Press, Inc.) Vol. 22, No. 4, 1996, pp. 49-70; and: *Access, Resource Sharing and Collection Development* (ed: Sul H. Lee) The Haworth Press, Inc., 1996, pp. 49-70. Single or multiple copies of this article are available from The Haworth Document Delivery Service [1-800-342-9678, 9:00 a.m. - 5:00 p.m. (EST). E-mail address: getinfo@haworth.com].

49

TREND NO. 1:
THE GROWTH OF DOCUMENT DELIVERY

It is easy to remember when document delivery was something of a novelty and discussions of it as an option were a part of every conference. Indeed it was only three years ago that the STM Publishers held a meeting in Amsterdam which focused largely on this topic. On the second day of the conference, five bona fide document deliverers, ISI and UnCover from the U.S., INIST from France, University of Leyden in Holland and the British Library in the UK, were invited to sit on a panel and describe their services to the attendees.

This meeting was a watershed event, because it convinced these publishers that document delivery was not only possible, it was inevitable. Up until that time, many publishers had felt that they could forbid the service and it would disappear. After that meeting, the talk changed from how to block delivery to how to price delivery.

Since that time, there has been growth in both the amount of document delivery occurring and in the number of companies or other organizations offering document delivery options. The British Library Document Supply Centre remains easily the largest document supplier in the world, at 3.1 million deliveries per year. Others of us are pikers compared to the BLDSC. UnCover, to date, has delivered about 265,000 documents. CISTI, in Canada, two years ago stated their annual deliveries at around 175,000. If we could count the documents being printed from distributed CD-ROM based services such as UMI's or IAC's, larger numbers could be tallied.

An analysis of the UnCover service offers some indication of what has been happening in this area. UnCover has been delivering documents since the fall of 1991. The service has seen steady growth since its introduction and now sees a doubling effect, on a month to month, yearly basis (Chart 1).

Use outside the United States has grown, with the number of documents delivered internationally expanding relatively rapidly in recent months (Chart 2). An analysis of countries using the service provides some interesting results; Australia, a country which is technologically advanced, presently accounts for roughly 68% of all international use (Chart 3).

The service is just beginning to generate enough data to allow some analysis of first time and repeat usage, at the article and title

CHART 1

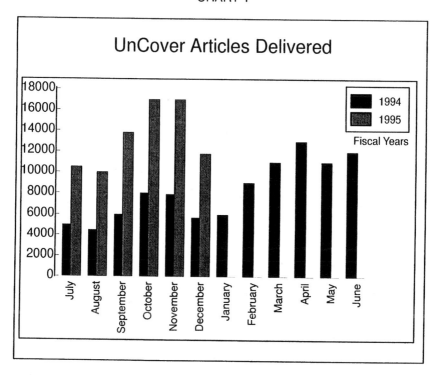

UnCover Articles Delivered

levels. The index today includes over 16,000 titles and about 6 million article citations. As mentioned earlier, UnCover has delivered 265,000 articles to date. As of November 1994, 19% of articles delivered were repeats, that is, they had been delivered before. In these cases, we had received permission to scan them into our article image file, allowing the second or subsequent delivery to be completed automatically.

At the title level, the "repeat" data is quite interesting. Ten thousand seven hundred eighteen titles have been ordered from three or more times; 3,125 fewer than three times. One thousand one hundred fifty-eight titles have never received an order and are not registered with the Copyright Clearance Center (CCC). These numbers do not add up to 16,000; titles which have never been ordered but are on file with the CCC eluded these statistics and another 600 titles (roughly 3.7% of the file) have been blocked from delivery by publishers (Chart 4).

CHART 2

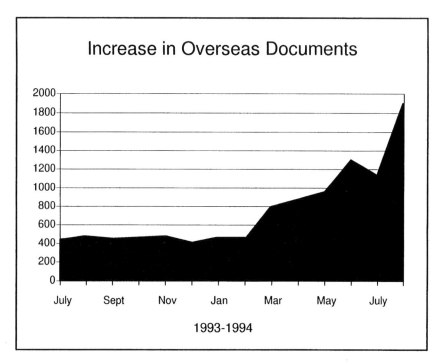

An analysis of current subject coverage in UnCover shows that 51% of the titles currently indexed are in the fields of Science, Technology or Medicine, 40% in the Social Sciences and 9% in the Humanities (Chart 5). A look at the "Top 10" titles ordered through UnCover shows a mix of subject areas (Chart 6). UnCover Reveal is the new online alerting service for tables of contents; a look at UnCover Reveal's "Top 10" shows several very popular titles at the top (Chart 7).

An analysis of cost shows that the average cost of a document ordered through UnCover is roughly $12.50, of which $4.50 or 36% is copyright. As you know, in UnCover, copyright fees are unbundled and shown separately on a per title basis. Average copyright fees have risen since 1991, though the exact amount of the increase is statistically skewed in UnCover because we established a default rate of $3.00 per article for any publisher for whom we had not yet received rates at the time the service began.

CHART 3

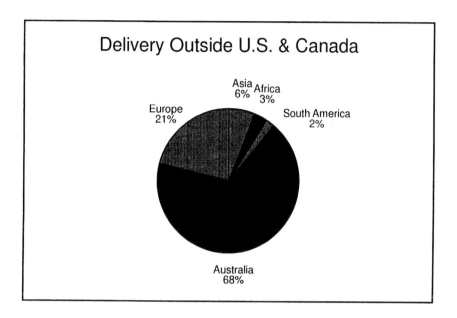

Delivery Outside U.S. & Canada

Asia 6%
Africa 3%
Europe 21%
South America 2%
Australia 68%

We do observe that rates for STM journals have risen faster than many others. The range of rates runs from a low of $0 to a high of $100 per article. We have seen all approaches to copyright pricing, including a penny a page to $5 a page. Russian translations of 3-5 page articles are now frequently charging $50 in copyright.

Of special note, UnCover is now paying more copyright royalties directly to publishers than to the CCC, by about 2.5 times. Large STM publishers account for roughly 1/3 to 1/2 of the direct payment. During calendar 1994, UnCover paid $500,000 to publishers for copyright permissions. The single largest payment was made to Elsevier; however, Elsevier with 1100 titles in the database is by far the largest single publisher represented. For the first half of 1994, the "Top 10" publishers receiving royalties from UnCover were: Elsevier, Plenum, John Wiley, Taylor & Francis, Springer-Verlag, Butterworth-Heinemann, Blackwell Scientific, Sage, Kluwer and Oxford University (UK) (Chart 8).

What do all these statistics tell us? Among other things, they

CHART 4

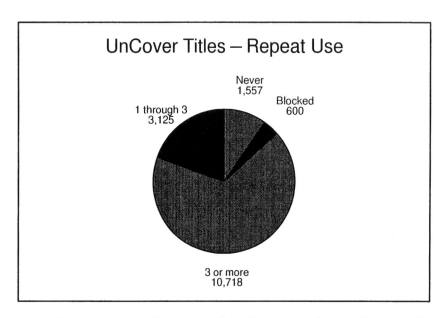

UnCover Titles – Repeat Use

Never
1,557

Blocked
600

1 through 3
3,125

3 or more
10,718

probably corroborate the generally held opinion that publishers will not recoup losses from journal subscriptions through individual article copyright revenues. While $500,000 represents a sizeable amount of money, this audience will recognize immediately that it is a small fraction of the subscription monies which have been eliminated from the budgets of research libraries over the past three years.

As to usage, the data appear to say that a large number of journals generates a large amount of use; that is, the usage is spread. Services like UnCover, therefore, must continue to maintain the current broad coverage of titles, and indeed, must continue to increase it.

TREND NO. 2:
ACCEPTANCE OF DOCUMENT DELIVERY
AS A COMPONENT
OF COLLECTION DEVELOPMENT AND ILL

Just as the STM publishers in Amsterdam in 1991 realized the importance of document delivery, so libraries over the past three

CHART 5

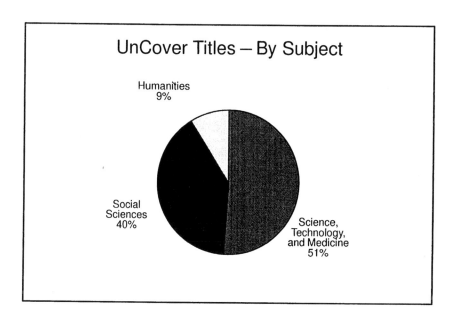

UnCover Titles — By Subject

Humanities
9%

Social
Sciences
40%

Science,
Technology,
and Medicine
51%

years have also realized that document delivery options can offer solutions to a number of plaguing problems. Chuck Hamaker was one of the first to analyze the benefit and has presented several papers, both here and at the UnCover Users Meeting in 1993, which provide evidence of the effectiveness of integrating a document delivery strategy with an overall collection development strategy, one which includes journal cancellation as well as maintenance.

David Kohl at the University of Cincinnati, in an upcoming article for *Online Magazine*, describes a familiar dilemma from the past few years. Kohl reports that:

> Through online searching and CD ROMs our faculty and students have a dramatically increasing knowledge of the universe of journal articles at the same time budget pressures are requiring us to cancel journal subscriptions in serious numbers. Similarly, we are encouraged, indeed expected, to pursue an aggressive automation agenda in the provision of new prod-

Chart 6

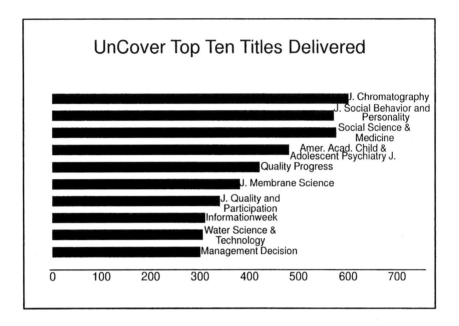

UnCover Top Ten Titles Delivered

J. Chromatography
J. Social Behavior and Personality
Social Science & Medicine
Amer. Acad. Child & Adolescent Psychiatry J.
Quality Progress
J. Membrane Science
J. Quality and Participation
Informationweek
Water Science & Technology
Management Decision

0   100   200   300   400   500   600   700

ucts and services while budget pressures are requiring us to downsize staff which is needed to develop and maintain a growing and increasingly complex automation infrastructure. How do we solve these dilemmas; how do we pull the rabbits out of the hat? (Kohl)

Kohl goes on to explain his efforts to work with commercial information providers to offer full text article delivery which eliminates the need to maintain subscriptions to selected print journals. Further he notes that these providers, of which UnCover is one, allow libraries to enhance their automation infrastructure and services without impact to current staff in creating or maintaining these additional services.

Cincinnati's $200,000 worth of journal cancellations took effect in the fall of the 1993-94 academic year. Kohl's article explains that the cancellation notices were accompanied with an announcement to faculty concerning the provision of online Table of Contents

Chart 7

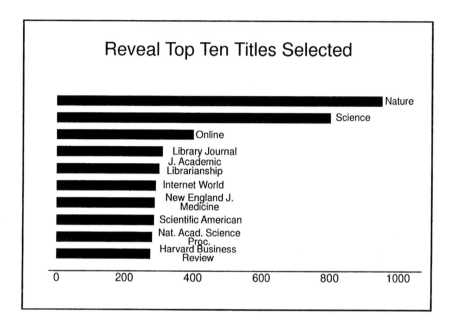

information from UnCover with free copies of articles from any journal titles found in the database.

The article goes on to report that first year costs were under $10,000. For the coming year, Kohl explains:

> This year, 1994-95, we expanded the free articles to graduate students as well (traditionally the heaviest per capita users of academic library collections) and found our annual costs are projected to remain under $20,000. . . . In short, for a cost of $20,000 we appear to be able to provide access to a much, much larger segment of academic journal publishing while reducing our overall annual costs by a net $180,000. (Kohl)

Mediated or Unmediated Delivery

Once the library decides to make document delivery an active component of its ILL or Collection Development strategy, the deci-

CHART 8

UnCover Top 10 Publishers

- Elsevier
- Plenum
- John Wiley
- Taylor & Francis
- Springer-Verlag

- Butterworth-Heinemann
- Blackwell Scientific
- Sage
- Kluwer
- Oxford University (UK)

---

sion to provide either mediated or unmediated use of the service becomes a critical one. For purposes of definition, ILL is an example of a mediated service; that is, one that requires human intervention. Services which allow end user searching, identification and order placement for a desired document are unmediated services.

Minna Sellers and Joan Beam (Sellers and Beam) from Colorado State University launched a project testing unmediated ordering through UnCover to their university community during the spring semester of 1994. In an article describing the project (submitted for publication), the authors cite studies which show that simply adding commercial suppliers as another choice within the traditional mediated ILL option serves only to add another step (or steps) and to slow down an already slow alternative. However, electronic ordering by the patron–combining access with delivery–minimizes mediation by library staff, increases the efficiency of the process and shortens delivery times.

For the CSU Project, links were created between the UnCover database, the Library's patron file and its serials holdings. A customized front end to UnCover was created which tied individual patron profiles to an institutional account. Profiles were created as users identified themselves to the system. Orders for articles available in the local collection were blocked; orders over a maximum item charge of $25 were also blocked.

Sellers and Beam explain that the service was available to all faculty, staff and students with a valid university ID. They add that users not in their current patron file were blocked from the subsidized service but could continue to access the database with the standard payment options. The service was limited to in-library terminals only, though they hope that network access may be offered at a future point.

Since UnCover delivers articles via fax, the Library reached an agreement with the commercial copy center located in the main library which charged $2.00 for each document delivered there. For unmediated, authorized orders, this $2.00 charge was the only fee incurred. Faxes delivered to designated devices in offices or homes had no surcharge.

The authors have provided in their article a thorough review of their project and the various modifications to the initial set-up which became obvious once the public began to use the system. In addition, the authors analyzed transaction logs and conducted a telephone survey to determine results, which are presented in a series of charts and graphs.

The transaction logs used by the authors included the university status of users, personal fax use, the number of requests by individuals, the total number of requests, and the fill-rate and turnaround time for each request, and various cost averages. A list of corresponding journal titles for articles ordered was also generated as a part of the project.

Results of the project are presented in the full article. With the authors' permission, summary results are presented here. Of the 281 users who ordered articles during the test, 38% ordered only one article while 62% were repeat requestors. The average number of articles ordered per person was 6.7 among repeat users. The highest repeat user ordered 24 articles. Graduate students were the heaviest users, ordering 50% of all articles. Undergraduates ordered 24%, faculty 14% and staff 9%. The spread of usage was thin over a large number of journals (this result is similar to that found for the database as a whole, as noted earlier in this paper). Seven hundred fifty-four titles accounted for all 1267 requests, and the average cost per article was $10.96.

ILL use did not go down during the experiment; rather it increased 25% over the same period the year before. The authors note that "Unmediated document delivery on demand must be considered an additional service rather than supplanting the ILL service." In fact, the authors found that as a by-product of their telephone survey to determine satisfaction with the new service, they introduced the availability of ILL to a number of users who were never aware of the possibility.

In the case of Cincinnati it is important to note that the free article offer extended only to faculty and graduate students, and was mediated through the ILL department. In that case, undergraduates were directed for their needs to journals held locally with no option for subsidized article ordering.

Expanded Service Options

Every supplier of document delivery services has endeavored over the last year to offer other added value options to libraries and ILL departments, based upon the various core services available. At UnCover we have introduced an S.O.S. (Single Order Source) option; this relatively new service provides the ability for a library or user to send in or phone in any citation, in any format, to UnCover, thereby eliminating the need for staff to pre-process a request or even search the database.

Cincinnati is among the first few academic campuses to begin using UnCover's S.O.S. service. Citations are sent on to UnCover staff who perform the initial searches and fill where possible. Articles unable to be filled are returned. By late spring, UnCover will offer options for onward distribution of these other orders, ensuring as complete a service as possible. The S.O.S. service was developed in response to the needs of corporate libraries who have taken advantage of the option since its introduction; however, a growing number of colleges and universities also use it as an adjunct to limited ILL staff.

UnCover is working to improve other ways in which it can assist the library, particularly in the area of collection assessment. For those with deposit accounts, monthly management reports have always provided account managers with the details of who and what was ordered; new options for gathering additional demographics have been added. For those like Colorado State who have established a customized access method or gateway to the database, usage from credit card users as well as from deposit account users can be tracked at the journal title level. These usage statistics can then inform local collection development decision making.

Cincinnati and Colorado State serve as only two examples of a growing trend. UnCover and other providers are already working with a number of other campuses to create similar tailored solutions. The importance of document delivery to ILL is perhaps best illustrated by the ARL's NAILDD (North American Interlibrary Loan and Document Delivery) Project, which obviously recognizes document delivery as an integral component of the full service. As you know, this project is aimed at improving the efficiency of existing systems, in the areas of management, financial accounting and elimination of redundant data entry.

Still, it is important for us to recognize that all these services continue to be based upon the traditional printed journal article, which is transformed, whether in a digital image format or in full text, for speedier delivery using electronic technology. These solutions, while effective, do little to alter the familiar cycle of information publishing and distribution. Indeed, they help to put pressure on a system which is rapidly failing. The more radical solution calls for electronic publishing combined with electronic distribution and like its predecessor, document delivery, this topic seems to be dominant in every forum within our industry.

TREND NO. 3:
THE MOVE TOWARD ELECTRONIC PUBLISHING
AND DELIVERY

Opinion on the inevitability of electronic publishing seems uniform; that is, all those involved–publishers, scholars, librarians, and middlemen like us–agree that this direction is important, will occur and will ultimately be very good. However, opinion on the speed with which the transition will take place varies fairly widely. As an illustration of the continuum of opinion in this area, let us consider in turn the statements of four industry participants who have recently written on this topic: Ann Schaffner, Science Librarian at Brandeis University; Karen Hunter, Vice President for Elsevier Science Publishers; Andrew Odlyzko, scholar, researcher and author at AT&T Bell Labs; and Peter Denning, Chair of the Publication Board of the Association of Computing Machinery (ACM).

Ann Schaffner's extremely well researched article "The Future of Scientific Journals: Lessons from the Past," takes, as its title suggests, an historical perspective to the changes underway in science research and publishing. In her abstract, the author notes

> From these [historical] models we can project that electronic journals must meet the basic needs that print journals do, that they will initially maintain many of the features of traditional print journal, that their transformation may be driven by external forces, and that they will be slow in reaching their full potential. (Schaffner, 239)

Schaffner delineates the core functions of scientific journals as:

- Building a collective knowledge base
- Communicating information
- Validating the quality of research
- Distributing rewards
- Building scientific communities (Schaffner, 241)

The article emphasizes the importance to the scientist of not only producing knowledge, but of making that knowledge publicly available. To quote directly, the author states that " . . . contributing to public knowledge is an essential function of science and the central role of science journals is to create this collective knowledge base" (Schaffner, 241).

Based on the core functions stated above, Schaffner concludes that the enabling technologies behind electronic publication will not be enough to bring about major change; rather, she believes that the shift to new formats will be slow and will depend to a large extent on the confidence of the authors and scholars in the new medium's ability to serve the goal of public knowledge, as well as on their confidence in the permanence and stability of the medium.

The View of a Commercial Publisher

Karen Hunter, in her article "The Changing Business of Scholarly Publishing," states in her summary that "Publishing is changing in response to economic and technological developments in the academic market and, over time, these changes will in turn have their own impact on that market" (Hunter, 23).

Hunter notes that consumers are accustomed to greater choice and flexibility in many of their every day actions, thanks to the advent of tools such as VCRs which permit the viewer to take back control over the television set. She confirms the focus on networks and other electronic media as a critical component in publishers' discussions concerning meeting new market needs, and she reports that publishers are developing strategies for utilizing these new technologies in order to convert present products to electronic form, to add value through electronic enhancements, and to cluster and tailor services to market segments and individuals.

It is Hunter's opinion that parallel publishing, that is, publishing in both print and electronic media, will be the dominant mode for the next ten years. She warns that, in this mode, the price and cost advantages which are being heralded for the new media will not materialize. To quote her article:

> . . . the total costs will be spread over the total number of copies sold, and the unit cost per copy or subscription is not likely to fall significantly. What parallel publication will offer is the opportunity to better tailor what is purchased and to add more value to the information at all levels. Some of costs may be locally recoverable or shared with other groups. Also electronic files should be used much more heavily (assuming desktop access) and the per-use costs should drop dramatically. (Hunter, 36)

Clearly taking the view of the commercial publisher, Hunter states that pricing is the single biggest challenge ahead. She notes the growing interest among publishers in licensing arrangements, which will allow published materials to be widely distributed and used, yet will compensate the publisher. In her words, what is sought are " . . . appropriate compromises between user access and publisher security" (Hunter, 32).

Concerning publisher security and copyright, her view is clearly stated: " . . . no publisher can afford to take paper-only rights, to concede unlimited interlibrary systematic resource sharing, or to ignore the conditions which will prevail as the NREN develops" (Hunter, 31).

The Scholar's View

Andrew Odlyzko (Odlyzko) in his now well-cited article, "Tragic loss or good riddance? The impending demise of traditional scholarly journals," takes a clearly opposite stance, one strongly in favor of electronic publishing, citing economic efficiency and more importantly, improvement in the use of information and in scholarship itself. Odlyzko predicts that the coming changes may be "abrupt."

He is " . . . convinced that future systems of communication will be much better" and speaks of the " . . . promise of a substantial increase in the effectiveness of scholarly work" thanks to, among other factors, the improvements in interaction and speed of communication which the electronic environment makes possible.

Odlyzko attributes the coming changes to a confluence of two trends: first, the growth in the size of scholarly literature, and second, the growth of electronic technology. He provides a fascinating analysis of the improvements in pure data storage capability which, according to his calculations, will allow the text of all the 50,000 mathematical papers published each year to be stored in 2.5 gigabits at a cost in the hundreds, not thousands, of dollars. As he notes " . . . it is already possible to store all the current mathematical publications at an annual cost much less than that of the subscription to a single journal."

Odlyzko's predictions are especially strong because they are based on factors beyond sheer economics, as compelling as his economics are. He notes the importance of the interactive nature of electronic publications, which he believes will serve to improve the quality of scholarship. And he points out the obvious convenience factors which electronic journals provide, allowing round the clock access from the convenience of the researcher's study. We have long quoted the mantra of "information whenever, wherever and however I want it," and Odlyzko's comments echo the importance of these factors.

The news is not good for publishers from this viewpoint and Odlyzko predicts an inevitably shrinking role for the traditional publisher. He views the role of paper as likely to be limited to temporary uses, with archival storage to be electronic for reasons of cost and access. Libraries do not fare much better in his predictions. To quote, " . . . if you can call up any paper on your screen, and after deciding that it looks interesting, print it out on the laser printer on your desktop, will you need your university library?"

Odlyzko sees a strong future for the review journals, which he suggests will serve as "gateways" to information in various fields, adding value to the mountains of information through descriptions, retrieval, expertise, etc. These roles sound very familiar to this audience and we may wonder why he does not advocate the librarian as a stronger contender for this "gateway" role. Perhaps Odlyzko's experiences with our profession have colored his views. Unfortunately for us, he suggests that " . . . a few dozen librarians and scholars at review journals might be able to substitute for a thousand reference librarians."

Implementing an Electronic Publishing Plan

One scholarly society, the Association for Computing Machinery (ACM), has declared that it intends to " . . . be one of the first to cross the divide" to electronic publishing (Denning and Rous). In addition to describing their plan for electronic publishing, the authors present first an excellent overview of the current process of scholarly publishing, highlighting those areas in which it is failing.

Specifically, they note ten areas in which the traditional system is breaking down, at least for this association. These areas are worth noting and are summarized or paraphrased below:

1. Most journals are now written by experts for other experts, but these experts constitute less than 20% of the readership.
2. Authors are increasingly dissatisfied with delays in the [publication] process.

3. It is an increasingly popular practice among authors to post their manuscripts on publicly-accessible FTP servers at or before the moment of submission, thus making the moment of publication precede the moment of acceptance.
4. Since the FTP server is becoming the author's means of dissemination, some authors now wonder whether there is any value in signing over the right to disseminate to a publisher.
5. The archiving function of libraries is threatened due to reductions in budgets at a time when both subscription prices and the number of journals have been rising.
6. Increasing use of online reference databases and document delivery services will eventually lead to the disintegration of print journals as pre-selected collections.
7. Tenure requirements continue to drive submissions to prestigious journals up, while readership declines, leading to "write-only journals."
8. Authors increasingly see their works as "living in the web" and view networks as new opportunities for collaborative authoring and for "dynamic documents."
9. Authors of works stored in the "web" make increasing use of hypertext links to other works rather than traditional citation.
10. Some authors are posting complete collections of their personal works on servers accessible easily using the author's name.

Taken together, Denning and Rous correctly note that " . . . the three key moments of the traditional process–submission, acceptance and publication–are no longer distinct or in traditional order." Instead of resisting this change in tradition, ACM is getting aboard. In this article, the authors explain the ACM's plan to create a true electronic environment for its published information, based upon "databases" and "database categories" which replace traditional journal identities. Membership in the association will include access to these databases of information and articles; this access will serve as the core service of the society. In lieu of traditional publication, "notices of availability" will be distributed so that readers can locate and obtain copies on demand.

Taking a forward looking attitude, the ACM states that it is looking to review copyright policies with an eye to encouraging use and experimentation. The article specifically discusses looking at the concept of " . . . copyright release to local agents, such as libraries, for search and print-on-demand." The association states clearly that it will view links as citations and will encourage their wide use; prior permission will not be required for authors to place links in their documents to ACM works.

The ACM document is truly an exciting one to read, because it moves beyond words and visions to action, and puts into place the sorts of policies and practices which will guarantee a productive and successful electronic publishing environment. If other societies follow suit, and clearly it is the societies who are more likely to be innovative here rather than the commercial publishers, then the fundamental improvements which Odlyzko describes can be achieved.

Personal Notes on Using Electronic Publications

In the course of preparing this paper, I found myself using electronic publications for the first time in a meaningful way. Granted, I am not a scholar and I prepare very few papers, relatively speaking. Still, just a year ago, in preparing a paper co-authored with Bonnie Juergens, I used online reference sources solely, but I retrieved (via UnCover) faxed or photocopied versions of all the works cited. This year, several of the papers I am citing have no printed counterparts (at least not yet), and one (the ACM paper) is only issued electronically.

Speaking personally, I can say that the ability to retrieve a full text work from my desk is a pleasure; however, some caution is still advised. Take, for example, the article "The speed of write" by Gary Stix which appears in the December 1994 issue of *Scientific American* (Stix). I learned of this article from an online newsletter and knowing that America Online features the full text of *Scientific American*, I was able to very quickly pull up the full text and print it. The article itself proved excellent, providing a strong, lay person's overview of the developments we have been discussing in the fields of publishing, scholarship and libraries.

Purely out of curiosity, and in part to ease the problem of providing a good citation to the work for this paper, I requested a photocopy (for personal use, of course) from a nearby library. Imagine my surprise, when comparing the full text to the printed copy, in finding that two significant charts including substantive comments and explanations, which appeared in the printed version, had no reference whatsoever in the AOL version. In fact, they were not even identified as "omitted" as is often the case in full text online files. I asked myself, does Gary Stix realize the difference? As an author, has his work been altered for the electronic environment in ways he would disapprove?

TREND NO. 4:
THE GROWING VOICE OF THE AUTHOR

Mr. Stix, in his article (either version), characterizes publishing as "bureaucratic." As is obvious from other quotations found earlier in this article, the strain between authors and publishers is showing. There is a classical tension between the two, but to date, each side has needed the other. The electronic environment may be changing that dependency.

In fact, in some sectors, war has been declared. In February 1994, the 4000 members of the National Writers Union and nine other free-lance writers filed a copyright infringement suit against *The New York Times*, Time, Inc., and UMI. According to an article appearing in the *San Franciso Daily Journal*, the suit (Tasini v. New York Times Co.) " . . . alleges that the defendants are distributing copyrighted, free-lance written newspaper and magazine articles on electronic databases without a license and without compensating the writers, who claim to own the copyrights" (Evans).

Tasini, who is President of the NWU, states that "The material is being used systematically and illegally." This particular issue highlights the variations in copyright law which apply to works created by free-lance writers, as opposed to staff writers. Materials prepared by staff writers are copyrighted to the employer; but, according to the Daily Journal article, in the case of free-lancers, magazines and newspapers have purchased what are called North American serial rights, which permit them to publish the free-lancer's article while allowing the writer to retain all other rights.

The New York Times and UMI are not alone in receiving attention in this arena. During the fall, UnCover and IAC were labeled as "Info Highwaymen" in an Opinion Editorial in *The New York Times*. The article referred specifically to the ability offered across the CARL Network through a pilot project with IAC to order articles from IAC's ASAP databases, on a "pay per view" basis. Following a series of discussions between the NWU and IAC, CARL was requested to discontinue this option. We did so quickly.

Thanks to this incident, however, we have begun to talk with the NWU and with other writers. It is our position that services like UnCover, which seek to pay copyright with each use, have the ability and the desire to pay the designated copyright holder, whether publisher or author, in a systematic and highly documented fashion. We can in fact provide the transaction-based financial record-keeping necessary to make these complex scenarios seamless to the consumer while compensating the rights holder. And we are anxious to offer our services to both publisher and author.

The issue is one for these two parties (publisher and author) to resolve, but that resolution may be many years in the making. As Karen Hunter made clear, publishers, both academic and popular, are tightening their grip on copyrights because they see the value of these rights in the future. Authors, however, are gaining independence and finding ways to participate in electronic information distribution without the publisher.

As always, it seems, the core issue is one of economics. What is clear is that authors in all sectors want their works to be disseminated as widely as possible and they want to participate in the electronic world. Whether it is the author or the publisher who will thrive in the future remains to be seen. What is missing from the equation altogether at this point is an understanding of the value and the use of all this information. If we do move to a less artificial and more demand-driven information delivery system, then these elements will ultimately determine the economics. We would do well to shift our collective attention to learning more about the use and value of these information documents; perhaps we can make these issues the "hot topic" for conferences two years from now.

REFERENCES

Denning, Peter J. and Bernard Rous. "The ACM Electronic Publishing Plan," issued electronically by ACM, Inc. Dated 11/30/94 (available http://info.acm.org/epub_plan.txt)

Evans, James. "Copyright Arguments in Cyberspace Lead Writers, Publishers

Into Court," *San Francisco Daily Journal*, December 19, 1994, p. 1 and 6.

Hunter, Karen. "The Changing Business of Scholarly Publishing," *Journal of Library Administration*, 1993, v. 19, no. 3/4, pp. 23-38.

Kohl, David. "UnCover Revealed: A Customer's View," in press, *Online Magazine*. (Text available from the author at david.kohl@uc.edu.)

Odlyzko, Andrew. "Tragic loss or good riddance? The impending demise of traditional scholarly journals," September 26, 1994. Condensed version to be published in the *Notices of the American Mathematical Society*, January 1995. Full version to be published in *Internal Journal of Human-Computer Studies*, and reprinted in "Electronic Publishing Confronts Academia: The Agenda for the Year 2000, " Robin P. Peek and Gregory B. Newby, eds., MIT Press/ASIS Monograph, MIT Press, 1995. (available ftp://netlib.att.com/netlib/att/math/odlyzko/tragic.loss.Z)

Schaffner, Ann C. "The Future of Scientific Journals: Lessons from the Past," *Information Technology and Libraries,* December 1994, v. 13, no. 4, pp. 239-247.

Sellers, Minna and Joan Beam. "Subsidizing Unmediated Document Delivery: Current Models and a Case Study," submitted for publication. (Preprint available from the authors c/o msellers@vines.colostate.edu)

Stix, Gary. "The speed of write," *Scientific American,* December 1994, v. 271, no. 6, pp. 106-111.

The Current National Copyright Debate; Its Relationship to the Work of Collections Managers

Ann Okerson

INTRODUCTION

Will tomorrow's readers be able to graze among electronic documents, books, and multimedia as easily as they have been able to peruse books at their favorite bookstore–sitting in easy chairs and drinking espresso coffees–before buying them (or not buying at all)? Will they be able to do the electronic equivalent of borrowing books from their public or college library? How can libraries make information available to their public as technologies change? As the copyright law changes? The answers to these questions are being debated today not only among authors, publishers, and librarians but at the highest policy and law-making levels of this country.

Ten years, or even five years ago, the topic of copyright evoked only a giant yawn. Not so now. The very word electrifies a gathering, and meeting rooms host overflow crowds. Today, the press calls our attention to the machinations of communications carriers, as they bid sums higher than any prince's ransom, to claim ownership of content to market on the Information Superhighway. The

Ann Okerson is Director of Academic and Scientific Publishing at the Association of Research Libraries in Washington, DC.

[Haworth co-indexing entry note]: "The Current National Copyright Debate; Its Relationship to the Work of Collections Managers." Okerson, Ann. Co-published simultaneously in *Journal of Library Administration* (The Haworth Press, Inc.) Vol. 22, No. 4, 1996, pp. 71-84; and: *Access, Resource Sharing and Collection Development* (ed: Sul H. Lee) The Haworth Press, Inc., 1996, pp. 71-84. Single or multiple copies of this article are available from The Haworth Document Delivery Service [1-800-342-9678, 9:00 a.m. - 5:00 p.m. (EST). E-mail address: getinfo@haworth.com].

1993 dogfight between QVC and Viacom for Paramount embodied the strategy that Content Ownership is King.

Why this new interest in copyright? Because there are vast sums to be gained–or lost–in the way that property ownership in electronic media is decided.

By the early '90s, the core copyright industries of the U.S. (including publishing, film, music), made up $206.6 billion of the nation's economy, or 3.6% of Gross Domestic Product. According to the International Intellectual Property Alliance, the copyright industries contribute more to the U.S. economy than most industrial sectors and more than any single manufacturing sector (including aircraft and aircraft parts, primary metals, fabricated metals, electronic equipment, industrial machinery, or chemicals).[1] The copyright industries (which invest heavily to bring information products to market) are vital to the financial, social, and intellectual well-being of the United States. Indeed, as the intense copyright negotiations between China and the United States suggest, nations may be more willing to punish other nations for economic harm than for human rights violations.

For the most part, the copyright industries create mass market items such as movies, trade books, and related items (the novel *Jurassic Park,* for example, spawned a major movie, videos, tapes, tee-shirts, toy dinosaurs, and other derivatives), while book publishing represents about 10% of that market and "serious" publishing about $1 billion, or 0.5%. That tiny subset embraces the scientific, scholarly, critical, artistic and literary record of human knowledge–a record we must preserve.

But at meetings of the "serious" publishers, exhilaration–about opportunities for multi-media creation and transmission, rapid information delivery, new products reaching new markets, and innovative marketing strategies–is offset by fear. A single sale (to a library or even an individual) could result in a document or product transmitted over the global Internet like an unbroken chain letter, ending hopes of revenue and threatening the existence of the publishing industry. Meanwhile, scientists and scholars see the Internet as breaking down barriers to information, which can be delivered more quickly and cheaply than through traditional print formats.

WHAT DOES OUR LAW ACTUALLY SAY?

Copyright law states that information can be owned. By law, authors or creators are the initial owners of their works–that is, they own the expression of their ideas (though by law they cannot own the ideas themselves), that ownership can be transferred or sold, and a market is thereby created, which in turn provides incentives to create and publish more information.

The current Act protects creative works in general, including literature, music, drama, pantomime and choreographic works, pictorial, graphical and sculptural works, motion pictures and other audiovisual works, sound recordings, and architectural works. (Patents and trademarks are governed by their own laws.) Copyright explicitly grants the owners of the expression of an idea five exclusive rights: to reproduce copies of the work, prepare derivative works, distribute the work, perform it, or display it. In order to do any of these things, one must have the owner's permission.

The current 1976 Act advanced U.S. copyright law in major ways. New technology continuously challenges revisers of the law, and the 1976 Act explicitly addresses technologies such as audiovisual, cable, and photocopying. In particular, the revision laid a foundation for the future by stating that the concept of copyright applies to "any tangible medium of expression, now known or later developed."

At the same time, the law recognizes certain exceptions or limitations on the exclusive rights of owners. Those limitations include:

- Public domain: covers works that are produced by federal government employees created during government time (Section 105); works past the copyright period, (now with exceptions the lifetime of the author plus 50 years); and those that are explicitly placed in the public domain by their owners (in practice, a minuscule proportion of any created works).
- Fair use: In addition, in extending its range to a number of new technologies, the 1976 Copyright Act was the first to explicitly address the balance between copyright holders' rights and readers' rights by codifying fair use rights (Section 107). Fair use allows use of copyrighted works without having to pay or explic-

itly request owners' permissions, for purposes that include research, teaching, journalism, criticism, parody, and library use.
- Archival preservation and the operations of libraries: Section 108 permits libraries certain privileges to preserve rare or frail works for future readers or to lend books via interlibrary loan, so long as such activities do not systematically undermine owner's revenues.

Thus, the copyright law protects ownership and at the same time places limitations on it, to achieve the balancing act that preserves the underlying purpose behind U.S. copyright law embodied in the Constitution: "to promote the progress of science and the useful arts."

STATUS REPORT:
CURRENT GOVERNMENT ROLE IN COPYRIGHT

The Clinton administration, determined to respond to industry and economic concerns and passionately committed to rapid development of the National Information Infrastructure, created in 1993 a number of super-agency committees to define problem areas (e.g., privacy, security, standards, libraries, copyright) and to make recommendations to assure full exploitation of the information super highway. In mid-1994, the 25-member NII Working Group on Copyright, chaired by Commissioner of Patents and Trademarks Bruce Lehman (and colloquially called the Lehman Commission), released a Green Paper or first draft report for updating and release in spring 1995 as a White Paper, containing a legislative package intended to update the current copyright act. Last summer, the Group put the draft into play and actively solicited responses resulting in well over 1,000 pages of written comments.

FLEETING IS "FIXED"

The Lehman Commission's Green Paper powerfully affirmed strong intellectual property protection in the NII. Indeed, few, if any, commentators disagree that works published in electronic formats and distributed through networks deserve the protection of copyright. Electronic information technologies qualitatively and quantitatively change the way works can be conveyed and, therefore, few if any current commercially viable publishers will have incentives to make their work available on-line unless the law gives them significant protection. Works can be enriched and value added to them in numerous new ways, and works can be delivered on-line almost instantaneously, it seems. If "Moby Dick is a megabyte" (a popular aphorism to help visualize its electronic size), then one person can send it across a network to another in a second or less.

The Working Group insists that the recommendations it presented merely "tweak" the law. The description is accurate, in the sense that comparatively few sections are affected by wording additions, changes or extensions and the fundamental organization of the Act remains intact. But in the eyes of many citizens and legal scholars, especially reader/user rights advocates, the suggested language overturns the balance that the current law maintains between the rights of copyright owners and users. For many who worry about tilting the balance in the direction of copyright owners, the Green Paper is most controversial in three key areas.

The first concern is in the Green Paper's unequivocal affirmation that any information alighting in a computer's memory, for any amount of time–however fleeting–is "fixed." The definition of fixation is important, because the Copyright Act governs only those ideas "fixed in a tangible means of expression, when its embodiment . . . is sufficiently permanent or stable to permit it to be perceived, reproduced, or otherwise communicated for a period of more than transitory duration" (Section 101). By the Green Paper's reasoning, copying occurs each time information is transferred between computers. Every chip is a (potentially) prolific producer of countless copies per second. The user who transfers copyrighted information between computers through a network, without permission of the copyright owner, breaks the law.

Another vexing area for users is a proposed additional right within the Act's current distribution right: the Transmission Right. The current U.S. Copyright Act says that creators of works "fixed in a tangible medium of expression" own the work they create and have the five exclusive rights within it. According to the Green Paper, "In the world of high-speed communications systems, it is

possible to transmit a copy of a work from one location to another. . . .
When the transmission is complete, the original copy remains in the
transmitting computer and a copy resides in the memory of, or in a
storage device associated with, each of the other computers. Therefore, this transmission results essentially in the distribution of a
copy of the work. The Working Group recommends that Section
106 of the Copyright Act be amended to reflect the fact that copies
of works can be distributed to the public by transmission, and that
such transmissions fall within the exclusive distribution right of the
copyright owner."

The Green Paper's proposal refuses to extend the Copyright
Act's so-called doctrine of first sale for electronic transmissions.
Section 109 currently gives the purchaser of copyrighted material
the right to dispose of (sell or give away) her copy. The Commission's recommendation follows from arguing that an electronic
transfer, however temporary, is "fixed" in at least two computers.
But one could imagine preserving the notion of first sale by other
means, for example, limiting application of the first sale rule to
situations where the digital transmitter simultaneously deleted her
copy, or working within the exclusive reproduction right that currently exists in the copyright act. Legitimate ways for lawful owners of copies of electronic works to sell their copy or to give it to a
friend, acts that are perfectly legal in print-on-paper, were left unex-
plored. First sale in the print on paper world is, of course, the
enabling mechanism for libraries to buy books and enable their
readers to browse or check them out.

Under the proposed changes, then, accessing works on-line,
browsing them, or transferring on-line works between computers
involves making a copy, one of the exclusive rights of the copyright
holder. Those who perform any of these acts without permission are
violators of the law. In contrast, the same use of information in print
on paper format, governed by the same 1976 Copyright Act, might
not normally implicate the user in any illegal action at all.

RESPONSES

Although responses were not always consistent, much of the
information-producing industry greeted the Green Paper's recom-

mendations with relief and acclaim. Their "worst case" scenario (in which the first sale of an electronic publication is the only sale, and thereafter all users obtain the material freely from the first purchaser) reduces income to the point where no incentives could exist for new intellectual works to be produced and marketed on-line. The additional rights and new proposals in the Green Paper forestalled this worry and appear to secure the industry's financial well-being in the on-line environment.

In the user rights communities (libraries, education sectors), the nightmare future is that nothing can be looked at, read, used, or copied without permission or payment. Library and education groups, as well as private citizens were voluble in their responses to the Green Paper. Many libraries are already feeling pinched as costs for information, particularly scientific books and journals, increase annually at about the same rate as medical care costs. (For example, the increase in journal subscription prices paid by research libraries last year over the previous year was 14%.) Libraries note that the cost of "traditional" (print on paper) materials is rising rapidly and the fees charged for electronic information licenses (when libraries and schools do not own material but license it from a publisher or provider) are even higher than prices for paper information.

FAIR USE–THE BALANCING ACT

If access to electronic materials without payment for every use is to be recognized, then fair use is the area in which the bridges can be built between the rights of copyright owners and information users. At least, that is where they have been built in print on paper. Fair use may not be the only possible bridge and it may eventually be replaced by other analogous concepts, but in the print information world, with its static documents and comparatively easily controlled bottlenecks (at the printing press and booksellers), fair use is where U.S. society has made much of the balance between users and copyright owners' needs.

Fair use in the electronic environment is hotly controversial. What is it, and how will it work? Other than stating that fair use should continue in the NII, the Lehman Commission said comparatively little about it, but it has fostered a series of meetings affectionately called "ConFU, "in which some 50-70 user, author, legal, and publisher representatives speaking for copyright user and owner interests meet each month in an attempt to evolve guidelines for electronic fair use. (The acronym harks back to CONTU–the Commission of the New Technological Uses of Copyrighted Works that officially met to establish guidelines around the then-new technologies 1976 Copyright Act.) In the Green Paper, the Lehman Commission challenged participants to reach consensus and to do so in time for the final White Paper. The Patent and Trademark Office initially provided the framework for participants to make a start and continues to convene and benignly shepherd successive meetings in which it became quickly clear that little agreement, if any, could be reached by sometime in Spring 1995, the time when the Green Paper became a White Paper addressed to Congressional judiciary committees with recommended legislation.

For many participants, the disagreements during ConFU meetings deserve to be cherished. Most publisher and user/library representatives believe the technology is not ripe enough to make much agreement about fair use guidelines possible at this time. They fear making deals before they really understand the implications of what they agree to, and at this writing it feels as if the process of reaching fair use agreements will take a long time.

STATUS REPORT–TEXACO

The long-awaited appeal decision in the Texaco case, a case argued on the fair use section of the Copyright Act, was handed down on October 28, 1994, seventeen months after it was argued before the U.S. Court of Appeals for the Second Circuit. The decision upheld the lower court in favor of the publishers. Previously, the lower court had held that Dr. Donald Chickering, a research scientist at Texaco who made single photocopies of articles from journals to which Texaco already subscribed and put the copies in his personal files for use in his work, infringed the publishers' copyrights by copying without either permission or without payment of the proper royalties. Texaco appealed the decision and was supported in the appeal by several groups, including a number of library associations, which filed briefs challenging the district court's holding.

The decision was made by the following logic:

1. The Court considered the character and nature of the use, i.e., Chickering's copying to be non-transformative and, therefore, archival copying. Archives, the decision argued, are the reason for which individuals and libraries buy subscriptions.

2. The Court considered the fourth factor of fair use analysis, i.e., what harm would the copyright holder suffer if this kind of copying were widespread. The decision strongly endorsed the Copyright Clearance Center and the role it has played in the development of a viable market for mechanisms to photocopy works and pay publishers. The Court noted that the case involved copying for which a license was readily available, thus implying that if a license were not available, the result may have been (or could in the future be) different. The case gives copyright owners a tremendous incentive to register with the Copyright Clearance Center or other such licensing entities and to the extent publishers do so, they will undoubtedly benefit from this holding that the scope of fair use may diminish as the ease of access to copyright works improves–at least in some circumstances.

IMPACT OF TEXACO ON LIBRARIES AND ACADEMICS

The Second Circuit's decision might impact libraries and academics. That is because in the appeal ruling, the Court actually downplayed Texaco's commercial use, emphasizing not so much the commercial, for-profit nature of the company as the fact that Chickering's copies were made and filed against the day when he might need to use them. In its least favorable (for library subscribers) interpretation, this ruling could suggest that making file copies of journal articles or book chapters by academics would not be a fair use. After all, members of academic communities copy for convenience and for the continuing education of keeping in touch with the developments in their fields–exactly as do Texaco's employees. The court's discussion of the "economic harm" factor

strengthened the basis for extending the holding of Texaco beyond
its context, despite the court's insistence that the holding is limited
to the specific facts of Texaco's copying.

In the original ruling, Judge Leval's emphasis on the overall
commercial environment of Texaco's scientists *did* afford a basis of
distinction with academic researchers. Texaco's researchers stay in
touch with the field to do better research which ensures Texaco's
profit. Academics stay in touch to do better not-for-profit activities
such as teaching and writing works which bring them no compensa-
tion but are done in a "circle of gifts" environment. Even though
the commercial environment of Texaco did not weigh as heavily in
the appeal, it cannot be discounted, for academia's greatest protection under fair use is its teaching and scholarly motivation. Working
through the implications of Texaco will take some time; academia
may now be more vulnerable in areas of research sponsored by or
conducted with commercial organizations.[2]

RELATION TO LIBRARIES

It is clear that proposed changes to the law, changes that
strengthen the control of copyright owners, will go forward and if at
the end of the current amendment process they are not balanced
with language that expresses rights of users, the way in which
libraries do business will be affected. Tomorrow's deluge of
information will increasingly be produced in electronic form, a
form whose owners' rights could be more protected than current
print on paper. As well, there is a strong possibility that the copyright period will increase to 70 years plus the lifetime of the author,
a development which will affect the movement into public domain
of all media, in order for the U.S. to comply with the Berne conven-
tion, to which it now belongs.

Furthermore, the distinction between paper and electronic information is becoming blurred, which complicates matters. More and
more easily, information that is not initially distributed in electronic
forms can be converted *into* electronic forms through increasingly
commonplace tools available to readers. Using scanners, scanning
copiers, scanning and transmitting workstations, and fax machines,
for example, transforms works beyond those their owners might

feel comfortable with or would permit. In light of the changing law and technologies, student, faculty, and other library patrons' information use activities need to be considered and guidelines need to be written (for example, for placing materials on electronic reserve, shipping articles across networks to fill interlibrary loan requests, incorporating materials into World Wide Web course pages or course packs, splicing expressions of ideas into users' own electronic or multi-media works). Very few comprehensive policies exist today in libraries or universities for managing such needs. Some university libraries are already offering support and advising their readers which uses could, in principle, probably be permitted under the concept of fair use and which should not occur without permission or payment. Although the fair use offers a conceptual framework, applying it fairly requires understanding of the law. Determining that permissions need to be sought or payment made, is often only the beginning of a long process of seeking and tracking down owners, a process for which today's mechanisms are still primitive.

In addition, electronic information is conducive to signing licenses under which libraries do not own what is licensed but instead they rent or lease it. How can such licenses be written so they offer the information to all the users that libraries plan to serve, and within those licenses, secure for them the equivalent of the fair use that exists for paper works today? (Likely such use is automatically granted under the law, but there is disagreement on such a position.) In order to make legally sound, as well as cost-effective, decisions about licenses, libraries will have to learn precisely who their users are for licensed works, how they use the licensed information, what exactly is used and how often. Indeed, if academic libraries continue to define their customer base as broadly as they do today, will they be able to afford the multi-user licenses that are the logical consequence of such a definition? If electronic information in academic libraries is accessible only to readers with campus IDs, then are academic libraries still "public" as they have been? Will they have the special rights that pertain to libraries in the Copyright Act?

In the brave new world of electronics, libraries are likely to stop doing a great many routine tasks such as serial checking, binding, and shelving but will undoubtedly substitute for those traditional activities with others, e.g., patron use analysis as well as comparison of license terms and prices, to make sure that the next year's license is appropriate to use. They will replace many traditional activities with services related to appropriate use of copyrighted materials.

The high-tech environment already poses many choices and challenges. Should collections librarians select conventional formats as a tradeoff for the greater certainty of ownership and fair use copying that purchasing artifacts gives us? Alternatively, maybe librarians ought to avoid buying and holding materials whenever possible, instead supplying access by the piece as needed and paying copyright fees? Collections librarians might opt to actively encourage a move to user-based and market-based practices–a strategy that could kill many second and third tier journals–and some first tier ones– whose articles are not read enough to justify the investment publishers make in bringing the work to market and libraries spend buying it. Such an access strategy would force new modes of distributing scholarly works–extensive deployment of electronic preprints, for example, would be one consequence, and conceivably only the better works would receive the value-adding services that publishers currently provide. Such choices put librarians in a position of power.

Scott Bennett has described a primary role of librarians of the future as managers of copyrighted property. In some cases, the library owns that property as large collections of paper, film, and other ownable formats. In other cases, immense amounts of intellectual property that the library does not in any sense own pour in on an access basis. What is the meaningful role for librarians in the second of these scenarios, or is there one at all? Bennett says there most assuredly is, for academic libraries are the special places where, under Sections 107 and 108 of the current copyright Act, users can exercise their rights under the law–fair use rights to do their teaching, learning, and research.[3]

Knowing the law and working with it to serve library users will be, if it is not already, an explicit part of collections management responsibility. Historically, librarians have defined collections management as a set of intellectual decisions by which sending money outside the institution brings artifacts into the library. Additionally, librarians are expending funds for information that could well bring no ownership of any artifact at all. Both types of transaction are straight swap of cash for service. An internal, companion activity now presents itself to the portfolio of the collections manager. It is collections development in the purest sense of the word. These days, everyone agrees that owning content and developing it to bring to users is a key activity. Where is such content made? It is made in our very institutions, and it too leaves the institution, to return when we send money out after it. There are campus committees and blue ribbon national panels worrying about who holds the copyrights of academia and where/how copyrights should be transferred. But that is only part of the picture; that is not my point here.

My main (though briefest) message is that today academic campuses all over North America are hotbeds of creativity, particularly in faculty and researchers' creations of important and potentially valuable (for research, scholarship, and education) information in electronic format. The creativity expresses itself in the thousands of academic discussions on the Internet, the hundreds of electronic journals and newsletters that college and university faculty create, the databases, the preprint servers, multimedia works, the World Wide Web resources. Who better than collections librarians to seek out the best works being created on campus and integrate them into campus networks and wider resources? To foster them, advise creators about their proper and legal deployment for the benefit of scholars and students throughout academia, to help guide them to formal publishers, if that is appropriate? For a long time, the best collection developers in that sense of the word have been the publishing community, who have historically discovered and developed the creative output of our institutions. By all means, let publishers continue to take a value-adding role for works that will serve wide, general audiences, earn them income, and supply academic libraries with created products for the marketplace to purchase or access.

At the same time, we know that the economics of academia and of libraries cannot continue to support the number of formal publications that are currently being created. Many of those, in the most highly specialized disciplines, have the potential to be distributed nonetheless, through the new technologies that have placed powerful means of distribution at our fingertips. If institutions can take a key role in delivering such research throughout the academic community, and if they can manage this information well, then we will all be winners.

FUTURES

Copyright over the centuries has become a tool for creating an economic system whose strengths and weaknesses we have learned–and must continue to learn–to live with. Many fear that in a new electronic environment, the old rules, sedulously applied by reasonable people, could have the unintended effect of moving the fences–suddenly, radically, in a direction few intend. Others believe that the new technologies are an order of magnitude different and more powerful than traditional publishing media, and that a print-derived law could impede the potential of electronic networked information.

The scientific, academic, "serious" publishing world currently comprises less than 1/200th of the copyright market. Publicly funded and created government information comprises an infinitesimal part, if any, of that market. By a historical accident, scientists and scholars are steerage passengers on a mass media ocean liner. The researchers, teachers, and students on this ship are far more interested in widest possible deployment of their work, whether in paper or electrons, for the cheapest possible cost. The trade/entertainment industry and the for-profit and not-for-profit educational/research sectors all make strange bedfellows who share the same law. For better or worse, the copyright law aims to accommodate all these very different bedfellows.

How we "tweak" that law and how we ultimately transform it will very much affect our information future. Even more, how we use the law to manage and control our own works will profoundly affect that future. Is it too much to hope that the lion may lie down with the lamb (on occasion), as widely and cheaply accessible public and academic information will coexist with information produced by publishers for wider and different audiences? We do have the potential, if we act wisely and well, that–if not all–then many, many participants in the new technologies will be winners.

NOTES

1. Footnote the IPA report (to come)
2. Footnote analysis of Georgia Harper
3. (LJ 11/14/95, p. 35)

Document Delivery in the Electronic Age: Collecting and Service Implications

Anthony W. Ferguson

Are we at a revolutionary juncture in how we bring patrons and journal information together? Is contemporary commercial document delivery, which combines access to electronic indexing and abstracting services with the ability to order articles with a few key strokes, going to replace both ownership and interlibrary loan? These questions, about the role of commercial document delivery, will be the focus of this presentation.

The degree to which commercial document delivery is used will vary between libraries, but it will be used[1] and this fact produces the need to address four other questions of interest: How should we decide what to access and not own? Who should decide the degree to which commercial document delivery services are employed? How easy should we make it for patrons to use this alternative to our owning the journals they want? Can the use of commercial document delivery services be defended as a good use of library materials funds? Not all of these questions will be answered definitively. The goal is to share how one collection developer is thinking about the process and to generate discussion with others about the role commercial document delivery should play in our libraries.

Anthony W. Ferguson is Associate University Librarian at Columbia University in New York, NY.

[Haworth co-indexing entry note]: "Document Delivery in the Electronic Age: Collecting and Service Implications." Ferguson, Anthony W. Co-published simultaneously in *Journal of Library Administration* (The Haworth Press, Inc.) Vol. 22, No. 4, 1996, pp. 85-98; and: *Access, Resource Sharing and Collection Development* (ed: Sul H. Lee) The Haworth Press, Inc., 1996, pp. 85-98. Single or multiple copies of this article are available from The Haworth Document Delivery Service [1-800-342-9678, 9:00 a.m. - 5:00 p.m. (EST). E-mail address: getinfo@haworth.com].

HOW COMMERCIAL DOCUMENT DELIVERY FITS
WITHIN THE ENTIRE SCHEME OF THINGS

Librarianship, at its simplest level, is a profession that seeks to bring patrons and the information that they need together in the quickest and most cost-efficient manner possible. From a collection development perspective, two problems prevent us from achieving our goal: First, the cost of this information is increasing faster than our library materials dollars are increasing. Second, the amount of information is growing faster than our library materials budgets are expanding.

There are two-fold reactions to these problems: Some put the blame on the commercialization of the publishing enterprise. This train of thought suggests that back in the old days when publishers were full partners in the knowledge industry things were better. That in that golden era publishers sought only to cover their costs, with perhaps a modest profit. But now publishers are greedy and full of avarice. For those who subscribe to this theory, the focus of their efforts is to break the monopolistic hold that a few European publishers seem to possess over the production of scientific periodicals. These librarians search for American publishers who will not be guided by a lust for the dollar. They also seek to break the monopoly by breaking publishing's grip on copyright. They also encourage the cancellation of journals in hopes that these profit driven publishers will move their capital to greener pastures. I think most of us in collection development have taken part in some or all of these activities in recent years.

Other librarians, together with collection developers from the first group, on off days from their battles with the publishing industry, have concluded that since they do not have sufficient funds to buy everything their patrons need, they need to stop providing access to what isn't needed and focus on providing access to what is needed. It is at this point that library practitioners seem to further branch off in two different directions: First, there are those who submerge themselves in a variety of client needs assessment techniques in hopes of becoming better predictors of what is needed. While I believe that we all have work to do in this area, the focus of this presentation is not on becoming a better predictor of patron needs. The second group of library practitioners suggest we forget about becoming better predictors of user needs and simply provide access to what is needed, when it is needed. In the cliché of the day, they favor access over ownership.

WILL DOCUMENT DELIVERY REPLACE INTERLIBRARY LOAN AS THE FAVORED FORM OF ACCESS INSTEAD OF OWNERSHIP?

For this, "information just in time, not just in case" crowd, two courses of action are pursued: resource sharing and commercial document delivery. I will first focus on resource sharing as a way of explaining why commercial document delivery is important. Librarians have long maintained their faith in the value of interlibrary cooperation. A librarians' manual composed in 1627 indicates one can "please a friend, when one cannot provide him the book he requires, by directing him to the place where he may find a copy."[2] Being directed elsewhere in 1627 meant then, as it did largely until this century, that the library patron would have to go to the owning library. With the advent of interlibrary loan, patrons are spared the need to travel, but they still wait while clerks at the borrowing institution, and a succession of clerks at the lending institution, process their request, find the needed item, send it to the mail room, have it sent across country or city, process it through another mail room, and finally place it on a shelf for pick up. Now, however, with the help of computers and electronic telecommunication, the amount of time needed to transmit large amounts of information has shrunk considerably.

ARL'S Ann Okerson notes

> we have lived for many generations with a world in which the technology of publication meant that access required ownership ... New electronic technologies allow the possibility of uncoupling ownership from access, the material object from its content. This possibly is revolutionary, perhaps dramatically so.[3]

We are clearly at a turning point in the history of resource sharing, but we still face significant challenges: First, knowing what potential lending partners own. Second, making the speed of delivery equal to owning the information in the first place. Third, expanding the breadth of materials available through collaborative collection development.

Significant progress has been made to overcome all three of these challenges. Twenty years ago, when working at Brigham Young University as an Asian Studies librarian, I participated in an attempt to cooperate with other smaller vernacular collections in the region. To resolve the problem of knowing what others owned, we exchanged catalog cards and each attempted to maintain little union catalogs. It was a sincere but futile effort. Now, however, for collections in all languages, knowing what partners own is a non-problem. Competing bibliographic utilities make knowing what titles are owned by other libraries a simple procedure. However, except for the bio-medical field, where issue-specific periodicals holding information is known through the federally supported DOCLINE system, we are still hindered from working meaningfully to share periodicals articles together in a non-commercial system of interlibrary cooperation. Before we can rely upon resource sharing to provide access to what isn't owned, we will need to develop DOC-LINE-like access for all subjects.

We have also made great strides overcoming the second problem: improving the speed and quality of document delivery. Fax delivery of information is now becoming as common as the use of the telephone. Moreover, there is an Ariel revolution going on in the field of interlibrary cooperation. The delivery and the digital transfer of scanned images using Ariel is becoming common. In addition, as libraries have increasingly focused their energies on improving the movement of monographs around state and regional cooperatives and allowing their patrons to order their own materials using real time computing, the speed of access to books owned by other libraries has greatly improved. However, the differences in speed between accessing an owned item and accessing an item at another library, is still too disparate. Interlibrary loan still tends to be treated as a poor stepchild to the other functions performed in our libraries. This is reflected in the amount of staffing resources devoted to interlibrary cooperation both in our loan departments as well as the scarce resources we devote to working with other libraries to plan and execute document delivery and collaborative collection development. Organizationally, these functions are paid scant attention. In many of our libraries we may have moved it organizationally from reference to acquisitions, or vice versa, but it is still bureaucratically far down the ladder in terms of attention and resources.

Resolution of the third problem continues to be problematic: expanding the breadth of materials through collaborative collection development. We have made progress but not enough. At the macro level, after having failed for centuries to get libraries to decide together what library A should collect and what library B doesn't have to collect, we are, nonetheless, still willing to put our shoulders to this wheel of rational but illusive work. As a Conspectus trainer I am conscious of how pervasive this tool is being used by librarians in search of expanded collaboration. For all the supposed weaknesses of the Conspectus, library groups throughout the country are using it to better understand their overall mutual strengths and weaknesses as well as collecting intentions. At the micro level, libraries also continue to pool resources to buy expensive sets, to create union lists of newspapers and periodicals, and to attempt RLG-like long-term serials projects. We just don't give up. But we still have not succeeded at making the perception or reality of access as being as good as ownership in the hearts and minds of serious researchers.

Let's now turn our attention to commercial document delivery services, to see how they have fared in attacking these same three challenges. First, let's look at how users discover what is available and the speed at which they can get it. In many ways, commercial document delivery is in a league of its own. Unlike interlibrary loan where the patron uses an index in one step to find useful information, in a second step discovers the item isn't in the library, and in the third step finds the interlibrary loan office to fill out a request form, many commercial document delivery vendors combine all three steps into a single process. At Columbia, patrons using UnCover conduct a key word subject search, discover what is owned and not owned, and order (using their own money) a fax copy of the article all in one process. In a recent pilot study, we found that UnCover was able to provide articles within an average of 27 hours. In an earlier study, 38% of the scientists surveyed at Columbia indicated that they needed information within 24 hours and 60% said that a one-week turnaround was acceptable.

In the third area, achieving greater breadth of coverage, commercial document delivery services vary in performance. Some focus on a core set of journals that will provide 80% of the articles that most of our researchers will require. Others utilizing mega collections like the British Lending Library, attempt comprehensive coverage. In either case, for most patrons, vendors are able to provide the majority of the articles actually needed. They do not provide, however, the breadth of coverage that is provided by the national distributed periodicals collection that can be accessed through interlibrary loan.

So if our job as librarians is to provide access to what the patron needs when they need it, what has this comparison of interlibrary loan and commercial document delivery taught us? Will commercial document delivery replace interlibrary loan as the favored mode of access instead of ownership? I think the answer to the second question is, it depends upon how easy we make it for our users to use interlibrary loan. As long as interlibrary loan involves the user in numerous bureaucratic steps, it cannot compete with user-friendly versions of commercial document delivery to quickly identify and deliver useful information. Interlibrary loan's breadth of delivery is superior, but that level of support isn't what is needed most of the time. Cost-wise, interlibrary loan is cheaper only if one ignores the very significant staff costs that are already built into our budgets. Only in the case of fairly high use titles is it more cost-effective to own than to access.[4]

HOW TO DECIDE WHAT TO ACCESS AND NOT OWN

If something is going to be used time and again, one should own it. If it isn't going to be used frequently, it is best to own it only when it is needed. This is not rocket science. Neighborhood rentals run on this theory. It just doesn't pay to own a family-sized tent canopy for 500 people if you have one child for whom you will sponsor a single outdoor wedding reception. It isn't cost-effective to own your own roto tiller if you have a 15' by 15' garden plot that needs tilling once a year. And it isn't cost effective to own a $5,000 journal for which you need two to three articles per year. On the other hand, if you go camping every weekend, you want to own and not rent a tent, and renting a lawn mower, for weekly mowings, soon becomes cost ineffective. Similarly, a core title that is needed for browsing and which contains articles of interest to large numbers of your users, should be owned and not accessed.

The problem for collection development librarians is to determine overall how much should be spent on ownership and how much to spend on commercial document delivery. With this information they can decide what titles to own and what ones to access. The problem can be visually illustrated:

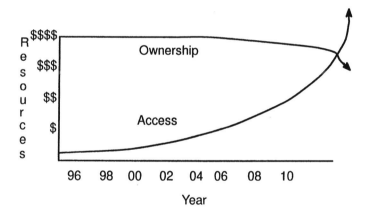

As time goes by we will all spend proportionately more on access and, as a consequence, less on ownership. But, what will be the appropriate mix? Will 75% on ownership and 25% on access be the ideal? A 50%, 50% split? Our answers will depend upon our individual circumstances.

Whether we increase the percent of spending for access using interlibrary loan or commercial document delivery, our solution to insufficient resources becomes the challenge or hurdle for publishers. Infrequently needed journals that are cut, attack the publisher's profitability and, based upon information provided by Joseph Fitz-

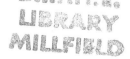

simmons at this conference, revenues obtained through copyright fees, have not matched losses to any appreciable degree.

How should publishers respond to our shift or at least the blurring of the line between access and ownership? Some publishers seem to have decided that the best defense is a good offense. Recently a student using UnCover at our institution requested 3 counseling articles from a journal Columbia did not own. Because of copyright fees dictated to UnCover by the publisher, a learned society, the cost for each article was over $100.00. Some commercial publishers have been even more aggressive. We are all familiar with the recent attempt by a European publisher to increase all of our costs by several hundred percent in order to prevent interlibrary cooperation. It would seem some publishers want to simplify the choices and make either option equally beneficial to their maintaining their profit margin:

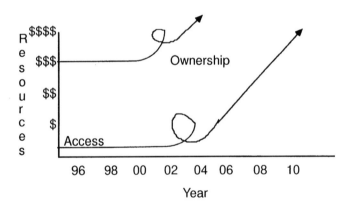

Consequently, deciding what to own and access will not be an easy decision over the next decade. Decisions may have to be made and remade as the costs of ownership and access change over time. The key variables, however, will remain the same: the level of local use and the costs of ownership and access. To make good decisions, the collection development librarian will have to be actively monitoring usage, ownership and access costs.

WHO SHOULD DECIDE THE DEGREE
TO WHICH COMMERCIAL DOCUMENT DELIVERY
IS USED?

For those libraries facilitating access to UnCover where the patron decides what to order and they use their own credit card to pay for the needed article, it is clear that the patron will decide how much commercial document delivery should be used. It becomes less clear when it is the library paying the document delivery fee. Even then, however, it is important to remember that the library's money is actually the user's money–it is just taken from the user's wallet or from the wallets of groups and individuals who give it to the institution on the patron's behalf, at an earlier point in time. Since patron resources are involved in either case, they should be involved in deciding what to own and access.

In the past, our universities gave us money to buy books and journals to meet the needs of our users. This approach was viewed as both cost effective and the best possible means of providing the widest amount of information to the widest group of library users. We engage the faculty, to varying degrees, in the process of deciding which books and journals should be purchased. When serials prices outstrip our ability to pay for needed materials, we ask the faculty to help figure out which subscriptions should be continued and which should be canceled. I submit that deciding what to own and what to access should be handled in the same fashion. We should be up-front in explaining the strengths and weaknesses of both the ownership and access modes of information delivery, and we should engage the faculty in deciding the degree to which each approach is used. Some faculty may protest or otherwise attempt to avoid making the needed hard choices but they need to be involved. To do otherwise will spell folly for the librarian who attempts to make these decisions for the faculty.

HOW EASY SHOULD WE MAKE IT FOR PATRONS
TO USE COMMERCIAL DOCUMENT DELIVERY SERVICES?

I would like to begin the search for the answer to this question by first examining four different journal information delivery models, two real, two somewhat hypothetical:

Journal Information Delivery Models

Cost	Traditional Model	Colorado State Model	Vendor Dream Model	User Dream Model
$	User needs information	User needs information	User needs information	User needs information
$	Uses index	Uses index	Uses index	Uses index
$	Checks library catalog	Checks library catalog	Orders document	Reads and prints at will
$	If unsuccessful, goes to ILL	Orders what is not owned	Receives document	
$	ILL borrows, or	Receives document		
$	ILL orders from a commercial supplier			

- In the traditional model, the user ends up at the interlibrary loan office when what they want is not owned by their library. At this point the interlibrary loan officer decides whether to use interlibrary loan or commercial document delivery services, depending upon speed and/or cost considerations. The library is in firm control in this model. This control, however, isn't free. Not only are the per transaction costs high, but the level of service provided is inadequate for all but the most patient.
- Colorado State University's library has streamlined this process significantly. They simply let their users automatically order anything found through UnCover that is not in its own collection and which will incur a less than $25.00 service charge. Patrons do pay for printing if they elect to have the article sent to a library fax machine instead of their own fax or e-mail address. This has proved to be very popular and there has been little evidence that the freedom to order direct has led to widespread abuse.[5]

- In the hypothetical vendor dream model, the user is allowed to order anything found in the index or abstract provided by the vendor, e.g., nothing is blocked because of library ownership or price. I term it a vendor's dream because it permits the collection of both ownership and access revenues. At Columbia we experimented with this model. We gave more than 30 researchers from the sciences, social sciences, and humanities limited funds with which they could order anything found using UnCover. We asked them to avoid spending their funds on items owned by Columbia but we did not place any barriers in their way. Users greatly appreciated UnCover and the ability to have articles faxed to them but they didn't feel title-only access gave them enough information to decide if they truly needed to order a fax or to expend the energy needed to find the articles in our collection. Until there are large numbers of full text journals, we won't know if users will accept this form of ad hoc ownership instead of the traditional ownership model.
- The electronic user dream model is frankly a computerized version of what most users have always wanted: the ability to browse or use an index to instantaneously read everything on their topic. This is why serious researchers have traditionally enjoyed enormous research libraries. They are not required to go through any bureaucratic steps to get what they want. They want, therefore, they get. Library research is fun when you can go from one reference to the next. In the electronic user dream library, however, researchers will not only browse tables, abstracts, graphs, conclusions, etc., but they will also do key word searches and, in the case of scientific journals, employ formulas or chemical notations as search terms.

Collection development librarians have it within their power to play a major role in deciding which access models will be used in their libraries. Are either the vendor or user dream models outside the realm of possibility for most libraries? Most of us already pay for, or greatly subsidize, the interlibrary loan and commercial document delivery access costs incurred by, or in behalf of, our patrons. The question is, how easy should we make it for patrons to use these services? Currently, we all employ punitive measures to force users to use our collections first, and access services last. In the past we rightfully justified this course of action because ownership was the fastest form of access and because we were unwilling to pay extra fees for users to order, and then browse, large numbers of items in the search of what they needed. New technologies, particularly full text journals that incur additional charges for what is downloaded or printed, will push us to discard or greatly modify our current anti-access modes of thought.

CAN THE USE OF DOCUMENT DELIVERY SERVICES BE DEFENDED AS A GOOD USE OF LIBRARY MATERIALS FUNDS?

This question brings us back to the basic role of our profession: bringing patrons and the information they need together in the quickest and most cost-effective manner possible. Can we defend the use of commercial document delivery as a good use, if not a better use, of funds to bring patrons and information together? One answer to this question is that it is as easy to defend this method as our current system of cannibalizing monographic acquisitions in favor of perennially increasing periodicals subscriptions:

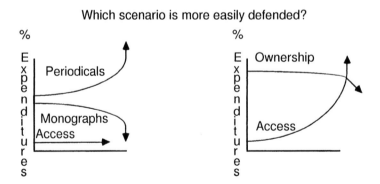

Which scenario is more easily defended?

The problem, of course, is that we do not live in an environment in which we only have to achieve the correct balance between periodicals, monograph and access expenditures. In our new age of electronic information we find we are in the position of needing to move money from all three of these activities to the acquisition of electronic texts and data sets:

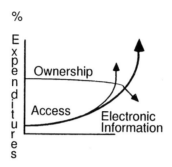

Determining and defending the correct mix of electronic and print ownership and access expenditures will vary from institution to institution. But what the collection development librarian has to be able to do is successfully defend the process used to determine the right mix.

CONCLUSION

Commercial document delivery is the newest in a succession of tools used by librarians to support user information needs. It will not totally replace either ownership or interlibrary loan. However, it is becoming significantly more important because of ease-of-use and speed-of-delivery factors. Its use poses a "need to communicate" problem with our user community. We need to explain the strengths and weaknesses of these new services and involve those users who will be with us over the long run (the faculty for sure) and involve them in the process of deciding what to own ahead of time and what titles to buy an article at a time when they are actually needed.

We must also seriously consider shifting resources invested in interlibrary loan staff support as well as periodicals subscriptions to paying for user-direct use of commercial document delivery services. And at the same time, we need to collaborate with other libraries to provide improved non-commercial access to resources neither owned nor available from the commercial sector. Whatever we do, we have to keep in mind we are spending other people's money. Our job is to be the best stewards of these resources possible.

NOTES

1. In a recent survey of ARL libraries, 87% of the 90 libraries responding indicated they were then using commercial document suppliers. This was a 13% increase over the 74% who had responded to a similar 1992 survey. Mary E. Jackson and Karen Croneis, *Uses of Document Delivery Services*, SPEC Kit 204, Flyer 204 (Washington D.C.: Association of Research Libraries, Office of Management Services, 1994), 1.

2. Joe W. Kraus, "Prologue to Library Cooperation," *Library Trends* (October 1975): 169.

3. Ann Okerson, "Synopsis," in Anthony Cummings et al, *University Libraries and Scholarly Communication: A Study Prepared for the Andrew W. Mellon Foundation* (Washington D.C.: Association of Research Libraries for the Andrew W. Mellon Foundation, 1992), xv.

4. Anthony W. Ferguson, Patricia Burch, and Daniel King, *Columbia University Scientific Information Study: Submitted to the Council on Library Resources* (New York: Columbia University Libraries, 1993), 34-42.

5. Joel Rutstein, Collection Development Librarian, Colorado State University, interview with the author, January 1995.

Collecting and Accessing "Free" Internet Resources

Julia Ann Kelly

With the growth of the Internet, collection development activities are beginning to broaden to include electronic resources, some of which are available at no charge via the network. Understanding them and finding a place for them as part of what the library has to offer is a challenge being met by many librarians.

CATEGORIES OF FREE RESOURCES

A wide range of resources are available via the Internet at no cost. They range from those that fit the traditional definitions of library materials to others that have developed because of the growth of networking and the unique environment that the Internet provides.

Many materials in familiar formats such as books, journals, newsletters, indexes and government documents have made the move from print to electronic format, and some of those that appear on the Internet from each category are free of charge.

Most books are protected by the copyright laws, but efforts are being made to digitize and mount older materials not subject to

Julia Ann Kelly is Special Projects Librarian at the University of Minnesota Bio-Medical Library in Minneapolis, MN.

[Haworth co-indexing entry note]: "Collecting and Accessing 'Free' Internet Resources." Kelly, Julia Ann. Co-published simultaneously in *Journal of Library Administration* (The Haworth Press, Inc.) Vol. 22, No. 4, 1996, pp. 99-110; and: *Access, Resource Sharing and Collection Development* (ed: Sul H. Lee) The Haworth Press, Inc., 1996, pp. 99-110. Single or multiple copies of this article are available from The Haworth Document Delivery Service [1-800-342-9678, 9:00 a.m. - 5:00 p.m. (EST). E-mail address: getinfo@haworth.com].

copyright restrictions. An example of such an undertaking is Project Gutenberg, which provides Internet access to works such as *Moby Dick, The Scarlet Letter* and *Paradise Lost.*

An ever-expanding number of journals are accessible free via the Internet. Some represent established print journals which are appearing in a new format, such as *Morbidity and Mortality Weekly Report* (*MMWR*), produced by the Centers for Disease Control and Prevention. Others exist solely in the electronic world. These range from refereed titles sponsored by mainstream publishers and societies, such as *Psycoloquy,* produced by the American Psychological Association, to much less scholarly and authoritative choices (Harnad 1992). Some electronic journals, such as *Postmodern Culture* and *Interpersonal Computing and Technology Journal,* were undertaken with a good deal of thought about areas such as their purpose, how to best use the new medium, and the variety of methods people might be using to access their journal (Amiran 1991, Collins 1994).

While most bibliographic databases available via the Internet charge for access, a growing number are free of charge. These tend to be smaller files covering a narrow subject area. Examples include the databases mounted as part of the Dartmouth library system: Cork, which includes references on substance abuse, and Pilots, covering traumatic stress.

The National Library of Medicine (NLM) has recently made the AIDSLINE database available at no charge for users who search the database directly from NLM (National Library of Medicine 1994). A number of files in the field of genetics are free to anyone with Internet access. Examples include Genome Data Base and Online Mendelian Inheritance in Man, both produced at Johns Hopkins University.

Under mandates to both become more efficient and make information available at a minimal cost, an ever-growing number of government agencies are mounting their materials on the Internet. Items include the text of congressional bills, census data, and reports, regulations and news releases from various departments.

Some government agencies are going beyond simply making text documents available. They may be adding search engines, utilizing the World Wide Web's (WWW) graphical, video and audio capabilities, and formatting material for easy importation into spreadsheets.

Some groups are providing free access to items that formerly had some cost associated with their use. In addition to AIDSLINE, the National Cancer Institute's CancerNet service falls into this category. CancerNet is made up of short (2-5 page) background documents on many types of cancer (National Library of Medicine 1992). For each type, there is a report for patients as well as one geared for health care providers. They are accessible via Gopher or by sending an e-mail request which results in the document being returned to the requester via e-mail in 10 minutes.

Novel categories of resources are also becoming available on the Internet. While some may not seem to be of interest to those involved in collection development in libraries, such as the archives of listservs and usenet newsgroups, others may contain information of great interest to library users.

The growth of the WWW and sophisticated software browsers allow users to tap into the multimedia resources as well as text. It is possible to view scanned images of paintings from a far away museum, fragile manuscripts, or radiographs of lung tissue. Instructors who have developed multimedia computer-aided instruction modules are beginning to open them up to users on the Internet. Connecting via the network to electronic bulletin boards which were formerly available only via dial-up access can save money. Archives of free computer programs have been part of the Internet for a number of years.

PRODUCING AND PROMOTING FREE RESOURCES

The unspoken rules and idiosyncrasies of the print publishing world are familiar to many librarians, and this knowledge allows us to carry on with our jobs more efficiently. Understanding the origins of free Internet resources is also important for librarians who are collecting and providing access to these items.

Not surprisingly, "free" Internet resources are seldom free to produce. The money may come from grants, such as the genetics databases from Johns Hopkins University. They may be incorporated into the daily work flow, as with a number of the materials produced by government agencies.

In many cases, free resources have become available at least in part due to the pioneer spirit that exists among users of the Internet.

Newcomers to the Internet may be horrified by the attitude of some longtime users who feel that all digital information should be part of the Internet and it should all be free. However, a somewhat tempered version of this feeling has helped make a large amount of material available at no cost to users.

The idea of the Internet as a new frontier not only gives some people the expectation that it will all be free, but it also seems to inspire some to contribute resources to the electronic community. Project Gutenberg, mentioned earlier, is run by volunteers and most of their budget and equipment comes from donations.

The Bio-Medical Library at the University of Minnesota maintains a resource called "Health and Medicine in the News," which provides the full citation to medical journal articles which have been referred to in the *Star Tribune,* the Minneapolis daily paper. It was undertaken to assist the staff at the reference desk, but has proven to be useful to other librarians as well as library users. Although most of the work is now done by a library assistant, a student and a librarian during the regular work day, one librarian contributes extra time outside of work and getting the project up and running took many extra weekend and evening hours.

Unfortunately, much of the information on the Internet is essentially self-published, so few of the free resources adhere to standards or deadlines or have quality control mechanisms in place. This complicates the task of evaluating these items, a topic which will be covered in more detail later in this paper.

Not surprisingly, very little is done to promote or advertise many free electronic resources. Groups with donated computer space and volunteer workers probably do not view promotion as a high priority unless they are hoping to solicit donations or additional volunteers. Their original target audience may already know that the resource exists, and aside from posting a notice to a few relevant listservs, there is no mechanism to inform the network community of the new resource.

RESOURCE DISCOVERY

Although the Internet is a 1990s technology, locating individual items on it may resemble the buying trips that librarians took to Europe more than 100 years ago.

Many librarians, especially those who work at institutions that have mounted Gopher and WWW servers, are aware of the time-consuming nature of the discovery of free Internet resources. Some libraries, such as the ones at the University of Michigan and Cornell, have formalized their procedures in hopes of streamlining the tasks (Riley 1994, Demas 1994).

Cataloging Internet resources is an idea being pursued by several groups. The Catriona Project, a collaborative effort in Great Britian, is looking first at traditional cataloging of materials on the network and next considering a plan for the day when OPACs will allow connections to these cataloged items. OCLC has recently received a Department of Education grant to coordinate the cataloging efforts of Internet resources and to include the records in their database. In a report about an OCLC pilot project for cataloging network resources, it was suggested that perhaps libraries should take responsibility for cataloging all Internet resources produced at their institutions (Dillon 1994).

Some print directories of Internet materials exist, such as the *Directory of Electronic Journals, Newsletters and Academic Discussion Lists,* published by the Association of Research Libraries (Okerson 1994), but time lags inherent in the publication cycle make it difficult to keep them current. Many how-to books about the Internet list a few selected resources, but these tend to be the more commonly known ones.

Valuable lists of resources in a particular subject area are beginning to appear in the journal literature, such as the current series in College and Research Libraries News, which has covered a number of areas from economics to women's studies (Morgan 1994, Glazier 1994).

Electronic discovery tools may also be helpful, but they suffer from the same problems that plague print directories such as currency and lack of comprehensive coverage. One gathering of subject lists in electronic format which may be useful is the Clearinghouse for Subject-Oriented Internet Resource Guides, maintained at the University of Michigan.

One strategy for keeping up on resources in a particular field is to monitor the listservs in that discipline. This could mean sifting through large amounts of e-mail each day. There are also lists devoted solely to new resources on a variety of subjects. Subscribing to one of these may cause an even larger flood of mail, with very little being focused on any given field of study.

The searching tools which exist on the Internet, such as Veronica for Gopher and Web Crawler for the WWW, are helpful but hardly allow for comprehensive searching. This is partly due to the lack of sophistication of the search engines themselves, which do not allow set building or proximity searching. The challenge is complicated even more by the nearly total lack of subject indexing on the network and the propensity of producers to give catchy rather than illustrative names to their resources.

Redundancy is also a problem in resource discovery on the Internet. Using Veronica to search Gopher or scanning other Gopher servers will often turn up the same materials over and over. It is similar to a scenario where 10 publishers print the same 100 books, plus an occasional 1 or 2 unique titles, and they make no effort to draw your attention to the unique ones.

EVALUATING ELECTRONIC RESOURCES

Many of the methods librarians use to evaluate print items are not helpful in making decisions about electronic resources. A large number of items are basically self-published or put out by small working groups, so judging on the reputation of the publisher is not very useful. Editors and authors may also be unfamiliar.

Noting that a number of other institutions have included a free resource in their Gopher or WWW homepage may seem like a good endorsement, but it may not carry as much weight as it appears. It only takes a small investment to add a Gopher or WWW link to a location, and many groups who maintain servers are more diligent about adding new items than about continued evaluation and weeding. Leaving a pointer to a free Internet resource is very different from renewing an expensive contract with a publisher or database vendor.

Self-publishing takes on a new meaning on the Internet. Many valuable resources are essentially self-published, or put out by small departments or organizations not formerly in the publishing business. It may sometimes be difficult to tell, too, if material attributed to an institution or company is the work of one person who is not really representing the parent body.

The longevity and solvency of the producer of a resource is important, but may be difficult if not impossible to figure out. How much staff time should you spend to check on a resource that you will not be paying for? It is reasonable to expect that a grant-funded project will continue though the life of the grant, but what about the many useful resources that are put out by volunteers or employees who may have many other tasks with higher priorities? Some libraries that maintain Gopher or WWW servers or produce network resources are beginning to rewrite job descriptions to reflect those responsibilities, but not all resource producers may do that.

A number of libraries such as those at Penn State and the University of Michigan have developed criteria to help in the evaluation of Internet resources. Some of the ideas mentioned are concepts that would not apply when considering print materials, including adequate instructions, convenience of use, evidence of ongoing maintenance and labor involved in making the item available. Others advise caution when selecting electronic items (Lynch 1993).

It should be noted that there has been some hesitation on the part of authors to publish electronically or to submit material to electronic journals. While there are the advantages of timeliness, ease of transmission and wide availability at a very low cost, concerns have seemed to center on the credibility and lasting influence of these publications, and are often motivated by promotion and tenure issues.

OBTAINING FREE ELECTRONIC PUBLICATIONS

With our mailboxes at work and at home filled with free materials we did not request, the idea of putting energy into obtaining free items may seem a bit odd. In some cases, connecting your library to a new free resource could mean adding a simple link to a Gopher or WWW site, and checking periodically to be sure the connection is still valid. Other items may take a bit more work.

For each way to access the Internet, including e-mail, telnet, ftp, Gopher and WWW, there are free resources available using that type of access. Some involve combinations of connections, such as electronic journals that distribute their tables of contents via e-mail and require the subscribers to obtain the full text via ftp.

The access vs. ownership debate also comes up in dealing with free resources. Is it wise to cancel similar print items, or electronic ones that are not free? Will the electronic version of a government document such as the *Occupational Outlook Handbook* take the place of the print? Will the producers of free electronic resources, some of whom are operating on a shoestring budget, take responsibility for archiving their materials?

TRADITIONAL TECHNICAL SERVICES FUNCTIONS

Although electronic books, journals, government documents and the like do not arrive via the Postal Service and require date stamps, tattle tape and call number stickers, many still should undergo some processing so that the library is able to maintain some sort of control over them.

Some items may "arrive" via e-mail, but many will simply be added to a remote server to which others point. A few may need to be fetched via ftp, either manually or electronically. If a library is offering local patrons access to these materials, does anyone need to check them in, or at least verify that they are being updated in a timely manner?

Claiming issues or sections of free resources that are missing may be problematic. It may be difficult to know if an item is late, or whether it is even appropriate to inquire about it, since no money has been exchanged and the publisher is under no obligation to the users. Without vendors to manage subscriptions and field questions, tracking down a small number of problem items could be very time consuming.

Cataloging initiatives, a few of which were discussed earlier, may bring new resources to the attention of a large number of users. It remains to be seen, however, if adding a standard entry to an OPAC or one of the bibliographic utilities will ultimately be the best solution. As with maintaining a Gopher server or WWW homepage, it can be labor-intensive to make sure entries are accurate and up to date.

ACCESSING FREE RESOURCES

Although electronic resources, free or otherwise, do not need to be bound or shelved, some scheme to present them to users in an organized and usable fashion is important. Many librarians have put their organizational skill to work building Gopher servers and WWW homepages. Trying to tame the chaos of the network by presenting users with a thoughtful and easy-to-use gateway is truly a value-added service, and many Gopher servers and WWW home-pages are maintained in a fashion similar to the free resources themselves: with little staff or equipment or time.

In addition to deciding which resources to highlight and how to design the interface, librarians face several other challenges in pro-viding access to free network resources. Gopher software and most WWW browsers are free, but the hardware needed to run them is not. The shift from Gopher toward WWW means that more expen-sive equipment with multimedia capabilities is needed to take full advantage of the visual world of the WWW.

The obsolescence of any of the software products that allow Internet access may not seem like a pressing issue, but the lessons learned by libraries who are still trying to support machines used to view older microforms should probably not be ignored when think-ing about continued access to older Internet resources.

Before library staff members are able to assist users with the Internet, they should have some knowledge and experience them-selves. It may be difficult to justify the time during a busy day to explore the far reaches of Gopher, but formal and informal staff training is becoming more routine in many libraries.

Gopher, Mosaic and Netscape may provide nicely designed inter-faces and be easy to use, but many of the resources that these gateways help users connect to may not be as friendly. Some assis-tance from library staff may still be needed, whether it is in the form of a person helping users in the library or answering queries by phone or e-mail.

Although the network may help to cut down on the amount of paper used in libraries, there still may be a need for a few handouts, pathfinders, and guides for novice Internet users. These items may also be easily mounted electronically via Gopher or WWW.

Some libraries have enhanced the presentation of free Internet resources by downloading them and dividing them into sections, adding WAIS search capabilities, or remounting them on the WWW. Government documents, with their lack of copyright restrictions and growing presence on the network, are among the common resources that receive this added treatment.

COOPERATION AMONG LIBRARIES

A number of cooperative Internet projects are being carried out or planned by libraries across the country. Although few have the main objective of gathering free resources, a number of them have that activity as part of their mission.

The Committee on Institutional Cooperation (CIC), which is made up of the Big Ten schools, the University of Chicago, and the University of Illinois at Chicago, have several Internet ventures either currently running or pending. They include the CICNet electronic journal collection, the Virtual Electronic Library project, which links the OPACs of the participants and enhances interinstitutional borrowing, and smaller initiatives by the East Asian, health sciences, physics and reference departments.

Other projects include Tex-Share, which links 52 academic libraries in Texas, and VIVA, the Virtual Library of Virginia, another cooperative venture by academic libraries. The Integrated Genomic Database (IGD), is an international project linking molecular biology databases.

NEW ROLES FOR ACADEMIC LIBRARIANS

Since academic libraries have been at the forefront of locating free Internet resources and making them accessible, perhaps they should take on the role of "collecting" these items for other libraries. Some public institutions have always considered the needs of their state or community in carrying out their missions, so making Internet resources available to the public is probably not a great extension of that task.

While more and more public libraries are getting connected to the network, most academic libraries have been using the Internet for a longer time, and are probably in a better position to collect, organize and provide access to free Internet resources. Few corporate libraries have the staff or mission to build links to resources on a just-in-case basis, but would certainly benefit from an easy route to locate needed resources.

Beyond other libraries, there are millions of users who are connecting to the network from their offices, homes, labs and schools. Any effort to organize the myriad of free resources would be a great benefit to assist these users.

CONCLUSION

Free resources abound on the Internet, from books and journals to multimedia items. Standards for production, promotion and maintenance are nonexistent, so finding and evaluating, and providing access to these materials is a growing challenge for librarians. Challenges are being met by developing criteria for selection, looking at cataloging options, and working in cooperation with other institutions.

REFERENCES

Amiran, Eyal, and John Unsworth. "Postmodern Culture: Publishing in the electronic medium." Public-Access Computer Systems Review 2 (1991): 67-76.

Collins, Mauri, and Sane Serge. "IPCT Journal: A case study of an electronic journal on the Internet." Journal of the American Society for Information Science 45, no. 10 (1994): 771-776.

Demas, Sam. "Collection development for the electronic library: Mainstreaming the selection and acquisition of electronic resources." Paper presented at the Symposium on Collection Management in an Electronic Environment, University of Minnesota, St. Paul, Minnesota 1994.

Dillon, Martin, Eric Jul, Mark Surge, and Carol Hickey. "The OCLC Internet Resources Project: Toward providing library services for computer-mediated communication." Paper presented at the Clinic on Library Applications of Data Processing, Urbana-Champaign, Illinois, April 4-6, 1993.

Glazier, Mary. "Internet resources for women's studies." College and Research Libraries News 55, no. 3 (1994): 139-143.

Harnad, Stevan. "Psycoloquy: A model forum for "scholarly skywriting"." Serials Review 18 (1992): 60.

Lynch, Clifford. "The role of libraries in access to networked information: Cautionary tales from the era of broadcasting." Paper presented at the Clinic on Library Applications of Data Processing, Urbana-Champaign, Illinois, April 4-6, 1993.

National Library of Medicine. "CancerNet and CancerFax provide additional access to PDQ statements." NLM Technical Sulletin, no. 269 (1992): 16.

National Library of Medicine. "Free access to AIDSLINE, AIDSDRUGS, AIDSTRIALS and DIRLINE." NLM Technical Bulletin, no. 276 (1994): 13.

Morgan, Keith, and Deborah Kelly-Milburn. "Internet resources for economics." College and Research Libraries News 55, no. 8 (1994): 475-478.

Okerson, Ann, ed. Directory of Electronic Journals, Newsletters and Academic Discussion Lists. 4th ed. Washington D.C.: Association of Research Libraries, 1994.

Riley, Ruth. "Maintaining and building a Gopher." Paper presented at the Annual Meeting of the Medical Library Association, San Antonio, Texas, May 16, 1994.

Document Delivery for the 90's and Beyond

Joseph J. Fitzsimmons

You've probably read many recent headlines about spectacular advances in information technology. It seems as if breakthroughs—especially those that facilitate the electronic delivery of documents—are being announced every day. But before we explore the recent advances, let's consider a spectacular document delivery experiment that took place a few years ago. It involved visionary people, a rapid transmission system, and the ability to receive a great variety of information. It also involved horses.

In 1860, hoping to win a government contract, the freighting and express firm of Russell, Majors, and Waddell developed a system that would carry documents the 2,000 miles between Saint Joseph, Missouri and Sacramento, California. The company promised delivery in ten days. This was half the time taken by a competitor, the Overland Mail Company, which followed a longer route through the Southwest.

The document delivery system established by Russell, Majors, and Waddell became known as the pony express. To provide fresh mounts for riders, the company established 190 way stations ten to fifteen miles apart along a route through Nebraska, Wyoming, and Nevada. The riders traveled about seventy-five miles each in a relay system. They rode under broiling sun. They rode in pounding rain. They rode in sleet and snow.

Joseph J. Fitzsimmons is Chairman of University Microfilms Incorporated in Ann Arbor, MI.

[Haworth co-indexing entry note]: "Document Delivery for the 90's and Beyond." Fitzsimmons, Joseph J. Co-published simultaneously in *Journal of Library Administration* (The Haworth Press, Inc.) Vol. 22, No. 4, 1996, pp. 111-123; and: *Access, Resource Sharing and Collection Development* (ed: Sul H. Lee) The Haworth Press, Inc., 1996, pp. 111-123. Single or multiple copies of this article are available from The Haworth Document Delivery Service [1-800-342-9678, 9:00 a.m. - 5:00 p.m. (EST). E-mail address: getinfo@haworth.com].

Logistically, the system was a great success. Financially, it was not. Russell, Majors, and Waddell, who charged five dollars per ounce for their document delivery service, soon went bankrupt. The pony express ended after eighteen months, in October 1861, when overland telegraph connections were completed.

The story of the pony express offers lessons for us today. Pricing policy, competition, and evolving technology led to the demise of the service. Those same factors must be considered not only by modern document suppliers who are developing systems but also by researchers who are evaluating their delivery options.

To evaluate the options for the 90's and beyond, researchers need to . . .

- Consider the types of document delivery available today
- Examine the benefits of combining outside services with in-house systems
- Review criteria for selecting technologies and suppliers
- Explore examples of institutions creating customized systems

TYPES OF DOCUMENT DELIVERY

A writer for *Information Today* noted that document delivery is a term that conveys different meanings to different people.[1] To some, it's the physical delivery of printed information. Others use the term to define campus-based delivery of locally owned materials. Still others use it to describe the supply of photocopies by interlibrary loan departments. Because of the great variety of services and systems available today, document delivery is best defined broadly. It could refer to any method or group of methods for ordering and receiving complete copies of original documents. The best methods are characterized by innovative technology, convenient access, and quick response.

The exponential growth of information over the past few decades has created both a widespread demand for documents and a full-service delivery industry. This new focus reflects not only a shift in strategic thinking among document suppliers but also a shift in attitudes among information seekers. In the early days of computer technology, everyone was excited by the unprecedented access they gained to information. Researchers marveled at their ability to search through thousands of journal articles in just a few seconds. But this early fascination soon wore off, and the Age of Access has evolved into the Days of Document Delivery–a period characterized by increasing demand for instant access to complete copies of technical reports, journal articles, dissertations, research collections, newspapers, conference proceedings, and government releases.

In ONLINE magazine's 1994 Annual Review of Database Developments, Reva Basch, president of the research firm Aubergine Information Services, noted that the rising interest in document delivery is helping to shape the overall information industry. She noted, for example, that both the document location and delivery processes are being streamlined because of researchers' need for enhanced online services offering both timely and retrospective coverage. She also noted that more people are exploring the use of "graphical and full-image databases, delivered via CD-ROM, the Internet, and specialized front end software."[2]

The growing demand for document delivery sources is being met by many different types of companies, research organizations, and educational institutions. For example, the Colorado Association of Research Libraries (CARL) offers UnCover, an online system that sends researchers complete documents via their fax machines.

In the past, many commercial online companies focused their efforts on providing abstract-and-index databases or, more recently, online full-text articles in ASCII format. Those same companies are now emphasizing their ability to send photocopies of documents via fax machines. As information-industry writer Barbara Quint has noted, "the online database industry has discovered it is in the document delivery business. It has found that full-text machine-readable data does not satisfy every searcher's needs."[3]

The DIALOG online service now offers SourceOne, an automated worldwide delivery system. It lets users receive fast fax transmission of high-quality copies of original U.S. patent documents and articles from approximately 500 business journals covered in the ABI/INFORM database. The nonprofit library membership organization OCLC offers another online system that provides fast fax delivery of articles. OCLC's rush fax service lets users receive faxes in one hour or less from FirstSearch databases such as Periodical Abstracts.

Document delivery services also include companies that house internal paper- or microform-based collections as well as organizations that use runners to locate articles in outside collections such as large academic and public libraries. Both types of services deliver documents through a variety of channels, including mail, fax, and the Internet.

An example of the former type of delivery service is The Genuine Article, a system created by the Institute for Scientific Information (ISI), which lets users order articles from more than 7,000 journals. Delivery options include a one-hour fax service and a "tear-sheet" service, which provides original pages taken from the journals.

Last year, UMI completed the acquisition of The Information Store. The merger gives researchers the benefits of both an in-house collection and an outside document locater service. For many years, UMI's Article Clearinghouse has offered fast document delivery from an internal collection of more than 15,000 publications, including journals, newspapers, and conference proceedings. Complementing the services offered by the Article Clearinghouse, the staff of the Information Store tracks down and ships not only copies of periodical articles but also documents such as patents, standards, government releases, and technical reports. The Information Store's motto is "If it exists, we'll find it."

Both the Article Clearinghouse and The Information Store offer customized billing options. Charges can be applied to appropriate cost centers, departments, projects, and researchers within an institution. Clients also can receive reports that help them analyze document delivery usage and prepare budgets. Recent record volumes of article requests from UMI's combined services are further evidence of the growing interest in document delivery services.

COMBINING OUTSIDE SERVICES WITH IN-HOUSE SYSTEMS

In addition to outside suppliers, many libraries and research centers have installed in-house document delivery systems that link abstract-and-index databases with images of articles stored on CD-ROM. The use of these systems through networks is becoming increasingly popular because network transmission speeds are becoming increasingly faster. For example, a network made up of T1 lines can transmit 1,300 articles in an hour. Using T3 lines operating at forty-five megabits/second, you can transfer up to 40,000 page images per hour.

Another reason CD-ROM systems are becoming popular is because the cost of storage is getting cheaper. CD-ROM storage now costs about $0.02 per megabyte–or the equivalent of five to six paper images.

Searching CD-ROM systems can be facilitated by using a comprehensive abstract-and-index file to serve as a "front-end" to an image collection. Widespread printing is possible by sending output to laser printers and remote fax machines.

An important benefit of combining document delivery systems and services is the ability to provide a cost-effective system that meets research needs "just in time," which replaces the traditional information-management model that involves storing documents "just in case" someone needs them.

Another important benefit is the ability to retrieve real documents from a virtual library. Publishers spend a great deal of time making sure that text, graphics, and page layouts work together to provide communication value to the reader. Sometimes, that value is lost when the document is translated into electronic formats.

The key to preserving the value is to combine full-image databases with computer networks. Full-image databases contain scanned, bit-mapped "electronic photographs" of original articles. Full-image databases combined with networks let simultaneous users receive complete information at local and remote sites.

An example of a product that combines both technologies is ProQuest PowerPages. It provides automated document delivery from one or more of UMI's full-image databases, which contain bit-mapped images of articles from thousands of general-reference, business, academic, and engineering titles. Updated every month, the images are faithful reproductions of the originals–complete with charts, photos, tables, diagrams, and other graphics.

ProQuest PowerPages combines the image databases with innovative document delivery technologies. For example, a specially designed 240-disc capacity jukebox houses the CD-ROM collection. Multi-site capability is possible because PowerPages can be linked to local- and wide-area-networks. Document delivery options include the ability to receive complete images of articles on in-house laser printers or remote fax machines.

SELECTING DOCUMENT DELIVERY PRODUCTS AND SERVICES

With the dizzying variety of delivery options currently available, how should information professionals decide which services and systems are right for their research environments? Sheila Walters, the head of Interlibrary Loan and Document Delivery Services at Arizona State University Library, suggests six basic steps. Writing in the October 1994 issue of *Computers in Libraries,*[4] Walters offered the following model for libraries and information centers that are expanding their traditional interlibrary loan services to include commercial suppliers:

- Assess needs
- Assess the capabilities of in-house systems
- Gather details on commercial suppliers and their products and services
- Evaluate needs against specific products and services and develop guidelines to compare potential suppliers (Walters noted that the guidelines should include scope of coverage, price variations, equipment supplied and required, projected fill rate and delivery speed, accounting and billing practices, management reports or other value-added services.)
- Test the products and services of selected suppliers
- Evaluate the services, considering not only fill rate, turn-around, and cost but also the ease of processing requests; customer support; and end-user satisfaction

I would like to expand on Walters' list to include some criteria applicable not only to outside document supply services but also to in-house technologies or combinations of both types of delivery methods. Regardless of how a library configures its system, there are three important issues to consider: connectivity, copyright, and comparative costs.

One connectivity issue is Internet access. Because the network has gained widespread acceptance in research environments, information professionals should consider the level of Internet access offered by any document supply method they are considering. UMI's ventures in this area include the ability to take Internet orders for copies of documents from the Article Clearinghouse and the Information Store. Internet users who have the Research Library Group's Ariel software can receive actual images of articles. Ariel lets users receive high-resolution article reprints right at their laser printers.

UMI has teamed up with other companies to make more than just journal and newspaper articles available electronically. For example, the Digital Dissertations Project is the result of a Coalition for Networked Information initiative to maximize the benefits of digital and network technologies while preserving the integrity of the scholarly record. Besides UMI, key participants include Virginia Tech, Cornell University, and Pennsylvania State University. Other organizations, such as the Council of Graduate Schools, are watching the project with interest.

The project will build on the existing information infrastructure of online public access catalogs, local-area networks, and networks in general. The goal is to simplify the dissertation process for graduate schools and give researchers the information they need quickly, affordably, and in a choice of formats.

To explore interest and technical issues, UMI mounted a subset of Dissertations Abstracts (about 5,000 records) on the Internet in May 1994. A server offered access to database text files in ASCII, Post-Script, or Adobe Acrobat formats. Though there was little advance publicity, Internet users have posted about fifty inquiries per day.

UMI also has posted a home page, accessible through the World Wide Web, to give Internet users a convenient way to find information about the company's services. We have seen significant breadth of access to UMI's Web server even though there has been little advance publicity for it either. More than 350 unique Internet addresses have accessed the server from twenty nations, including

Russia, Kuwait, Poland, Italy, Norway, Austria, and New Zealand. About seventy-five percent of the use has come from academic sites, but we also have seen activity from government agencies such as NASA as well as corporations such as Boeing, Xerox, and Intel.

Another connectivity issue is interoperability; document delivery is optimized when all of the organization's systems and services work together. A technological standard facilitating interoperability is Z39.50, which was put forth by the American National Standards Institute. Z39.50 lets searchers use the same commands to search different databases–even when they have different structures and need to be accessed through different servers. Many organizations are making creative use of the standard to enhance their information systems. For example, the University of New Brunswick has combined World Wide Web technology with a local Z39.50 server to create a hypertext link between images of articles stored on CD-ROM and the ABI/INFORM business database of abstract-and-index records.[5]

Document suppliers who address connectivity issues such as Internet access and interoperability can provide dynamic collections of information. Of course, the fact that today's documents can be manipulated electronically brings up new copyright questions. Information technologies make it easy for anyone to copy, archive, or distribute information without permission. Some industry observers have predicted that technology will make copyright law virtually useless, but I disagree. I believe electronic publishers have a responsibility to protect copyright.

UMI's policies and systems for protecting copyright in an electronic environment include a system called BART (Billing and Royalty Tracking), which handles copyright compliance for the ProQuest CD-ROM databases of full-image journal articles. BART tracks usage and provides reports to system administrators as well as a detailed annual report to publishers. Through direct agreements with thousands of publishers and authors, UMI also ensures that every document available through the Article Clearinghouse is 100 percent copyright cleared, and there is no additional copyright charge to the researcher.

The cost of document delivery is another critical issue–especially in these days when budgets are being cut and resources are stretched to the limit. With so many document options from which to choose, information professionals need to compare costs to make sure they are getting the most value for their money. The average cost of a traditional print serial subscription is $130. According to an ARL/RLG study, the average interlibrary loan transaction is $29.55. The average cost per document from a commercial supplier is $15.00–about half the cost of interlibrary loan.

Many information centers can further reduce costs by installing an in-house CD-ROM-based image system. Of course, the cost per transaction with such a system is highly variable. It depends on the database leased, the hardware needed, the cost of supplies such as printer paper and toner cartridges, and the number of articles printed per day. If you consider that it costs $19,120 per year to lease the Global Edition of Business Periodicals Ondisc, which contains cover-to-cover article images for more than 500 journals (as well as abstracting and indexing for an additional 500 publications), then you can estimate your article costs based on the expected volume of requests.

Clearly, libraries can optimize cost savings and provide access to a comprehensive collection of journal articles by using in-house technologies for the most popular material and outside suppliers for less frequently requested documents.

To help libraries streamline both delivery methods, UMI is developing a client-server technology with a unique pricing structure. But before we take a look at that system, let's consider a few organizations that have combined technologies to create customized systems that meet their specific research needs.

CUSTOMIZED DOCUMENT DELIVERY SYSTEMS

An example of an academic institution that combines in-house systems with outside services is the Hong Kong University of Science and Technology. The library at this institution offers not only extensive microform collections but also more than seventy electronic databases. Thirty are available on the library's CD-ROM network, which encompasses 120 drives. Collectively, the library's electronic databases offer patrons access to more than 50,000 journals. Min-Min Chang, the library's director, installed the first INNO-

PAC, an integrated online library system, outside the United States. The system offers an English, Chinese, Japanese, and Korean interface. For any documents not available in the library's electronic databases, library patrons can use the supplemental services of such suppliers as UnCover, the Article Clearinghouse, OCLC, and The British Document Supply Centre.

Another innovative document delivery solution is being put in place at Cornell University. The Chemistry Online Retrieval Experiment (CORE) premiered at Cornell University in April 1993. CORE offers chemists at Cornell access to not only the text but also the graphics in more than twenty American Chemical Society journals. The system is a joint venture involving Cornell, the American Chemical Society, OCLC, and Bellcore.

CORE eventually will date back to 1980 for most journals and represent a paper collection that would take up more than 600 feet of shelf space.

To ease the process of putting that amount of data online, the journals are produced by the publisher with software that sets the appearance of the printed page. Raw data such as formatting codes, text, tables, and small graphics are recorded so they can be displayed on a desktop monitor and sent to the library. Detailed graphical images are scanned separately and kept as compressed files on optical storage disks. In the library, a researcher uses a graphical interface to activate OCLC's search program, which scans the data for key words. A list of matching articles pops up in a window, the user chooses a title, and images appear on-screen.

In an article about the CORE project, the journal *Science* noted that being able to get the whole paper online could revolutionize the way scientists keep up with literature. Cornell Library Director Jan Olsen told *Science* that "CORE will bring a journal to them when they want it, where they want it, and as often as they want it, whether or not someone else is using it. . . . It's a better job of keeping up than they can do if they have to physically eyeball all the literature every time they want something."[6]

Another document delivery project developed in a large academic environment is the one in place at OHIOLINK, a state-wide consortium of seventeen colleges and universities and the State Library of Ohio. They have created an information system, based on the PowerPages technology, which enables patrons to make direct requests for documents from any site in the consortium. The system provides instant turnaround of requested documents and remote printing at sites all over Ohio.

But it's not just large academic institutions using full-image technologies that are creating innovative document delivery systems. For example, Howard Community College in Columbia, Maryland has put together a system of network and CD-ROM technologies that gives the students instant access to thousands of journal citations and several million complete articles. Students access the network through ten computer workstations located throughout the library's main floor. Several databases are available, including three full-text ASCII-based newspaper files, *The New York Times, The Wall Street Journal,* and *The Washington Post.* One of the most popular databases is General Periodicals Ondisc (GPO), which offers abstracting for articles published in more than 1,500 general-interest magazines. It also provides complete images of articles published in more than 400 key publications.

Besides academic institutions, hundreds of corporate and public libraries are creating customized document delivery systems as well.

To facilitate the creation of customized systems, UMI is developing a service called ADDS (Advanced Document Delivery System). Based on a client-server technology, it will enhance any type or size library's mix of in-house systems and outside suppliers. When it is completed, researchers will be able to access UMI's electronic holdings–including databases of abstracts, ASCII full text, and bit-mapped full-image articles (initially more than nine million page images)–from the data center at UMI headquarters in Ann Arbor, Michigan. It will be the first system to allow researchers to view actual article images in remote settings before electing to print the complete document.

ADDS will be accessible through dedicated communication lines or by dialing in through a modem using standard telephone lines. The communication backbone for the system will let researchers establish a high-speed connection, which can include dedicated Wide-Area-Network connections operating at Local-Area-Network speeds. The ADDS client software is fully compliant with the TCP/IP communication standard. That means researchers will have the choice of using a private connection, the Internet, or a value-added network service as their Wide-Area-Network link to the system. Pricing options will include subscription pricing on a per-simulta-neous-user basis, which covers the cost of any needed documents within a collection of information in the system. Another option—transaction pricing—will let users search and pay by the individual document. The cost of the document will depend on the format needed: abstract only, ASCII full text, full image, or a new "UMI format"—a combination of enhanced ASCII text and images (the best of both worlds). Searching the system and identifying a list of documents will be free, with the exception of any telecommunications charge.

ADDS will be released in beta test by May 1. Work on it will continue throughout the summer. Full commercial release is scheduled for this fall. When it is complete, ADDS will offer the depth and range of coverage to make it suitable as a primary information system in many research environments, but it also complements other document delivery products and services. If a library has extensive microfilm or microfiche holdings, ADDS will offer access to complementary material from the most extensive collection of information maintained by any organization other than the Library of Congress. If a library uses databases on magnetic tapes loaded on a mainframe computer, ADDS will offer easy access to cost-effective article images. If a library already has images on CD-ROMs, ADDS will fill gaps by providing a direct route to infrequently used or difficult-to-find material that is not covered by other in-house systems or outside services.

Whatever the mix of resources, ADDS will provide unprecedented access to information, and every document will have full copyright clearance.

DOCUMENT DELIVERY FOR THE FUTURE

The continuing evolution of information technology will sustain the development of innovative document delivery products and services. Further advances in imaging technology, data storage media, compression techniques, and computer networks will facilitate the creation of systems that serve increasing numbers of people in many different types of research environments.

A key to successfully implementing effective document delivery systems is collaboration. If print publishers, electronic database producers, technology companies, librarians, researchers, and other information professionals work together, the result will be a wealth of documents available in a variety of formats. This will enhance everyone's ability to find information, create knowledge, and share it with colleagues around the world.

NOTES

1. Jackson, Mary E. "Dissecting Document Delivery." *Information Today* 11, no. 10 (November 1994): 44-45.

2. Basch, Reva. "Annual Review of Database Developments." *DATABASE* 17, no. 6 (December 1994): 14-16.

3. Quint, Barbara. "The Document Delivery Business." *Wilson Library Bulletin* 69, no. 1 (September 1994): 70-71.

4. Walters, Sheila. "Commercial Document Delivery: Vendor Selection Criteria." *Computers in Libraries* 14, no. 9 (October 1994): 14-16.

5. Cunningham, David; Sloan, Stephen. "An Enhanced Z39.50 Gateway to the WorldWideWeb." *Computers in Libraries* 14, no. 9 (October 1994): 20-22.

6. Krumenaker, Larry. "Virtual Libraries, Complete with Journals, Get Real." *Science* 260, no. 5111 (May 21, 1993): 1066-1067.

Index

The letter f following a page number indicates a figure.

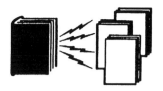

Haworth
DOCUMENT DELIVERY
SERVICE

This valuable service provides a single-article order form for any article from a Haworth journal.

- *Time Saving:* No running around from library to library to find a specific article.
- *Cost Effective:* All costs are kept down to a minimum.
- *Fast Delivery:* Choose from several options, including same-day FAX.
- *No Copyright Hassles:* You will be supplied by the original publisher.
- *Easy Payment:* Choose from several easy payment methods.

Open Accounts Welcome for . . .
- Library Interlibrary Loan Departments
- Library Network/Consortia Wishing to Provide Single-Article Services
- Indexing/Abstracting Services with Single Article Provision Services
- Document Provision Brokers and Freelance Information Service Providers

---

MAIL or *FAX* THIS ENTIRE ORDER FORM TO:

Haworth Document Delivery Service	**or FAX:** 1-800-895-0582
The Haworth Press, Inc.	**or CALL:** 1-800-342-9678
10 Alice Street	9am-5pm EST
Binghamton, NY 13904-1580	

PLEASE SEND ME PHOTOCOPIES OF THE FOLLOWING SINGLE ARTICLES:

1) Journal Title: _____

   Vol/Issue/Year: _____ Starting & Ending Pages: _____

Article Title: _____

---

2) Journal Title: _____

   Vol/Issue/Year: _____ Starting & Ending Pages: _____

Article Title: _____

---

3) Journal Title: _____

   Vol/Issue/Year: _____ Starting & Ending Pages: _____

Article Title: _____

---

4) Journal Title: _____

   Vol/Issue/Year: _____ Starting & Ending Pages: _____

Article Title: _____

(See other side for Costs and Payment Information)

COSTS: Please figure your cost to order quality copies of an article.

1. Set-up charge per article: $8.00

              ($8.00 × number of separate articles) _____

2. Photocopying charge for each article:

              1-10 pages: $1.00 _____

              11-19 pages: $3.00 _____

              20-29 pages: $5.00 _____

              30+ pages: $2.00/10 pages _____

3. Flexicover (optional): $2.00/article _____

4. Postage & Handling: US: $1.00 for the first article/

              $.50 each additional article _____

              Federal Express: $25.00 _____

              Outside US: $2.00 for first article/

              $.50 each additional article _____

5. Same-day FAX service: $.35 per page _____

GRAND TOTAL: _____

METHOD OF PAYMENT: (please check one)

❑ Check enclosed ❑ Please ship and bill. PO # _____

         (sorry we can ship and bill to bookstores only! All others must pre-pay)

❑ Charge to my credit card: ❑ Visa; ❑ MasterCard; ❑ Discover;

            ❑ American Express;

Account Number: _____ Expiration date: _____

Signature: ✗ _____

Name: _____ Institution: _____

Address: _____

_____

City: _____ State: _____ Zip: _____

Phone Number: _____ FAX Number: _____

MAIL or *FAX* THIS ENTIRE ORDER FORM TO:

Haworth Document Delivery Service	**or FAX:** 1-800-895-0582
The Haworth Press, Inc.	**or CALL:** 1-800-342-9678
10 Alice Street	9am-5pm EST)
Binghamton, NY 13904-1580	